THE WRITER'S
ADVENTURE
GUIDE

BOOKS BY BETH BARANY
Overcome Writer's Block
The Writer's Adventure Guide

HOME-STUDY COURSES
The Writer's Adventure Guide E-course
The Writer's Motivation E-course

CARD DECK
The Writer's Tarot

CONTRIBUTOR
Writing Romance: The Ultimate Guide on Craft, Creation, and
Industry Connections

The Writer's
ADVENTURE
Guide

12 Stages to
Writing Your Book

Beth Barany

BARANY PUBLISHING

Oakland, CA

Published by Barany Publishing, 771 Kingston Ave., #108, Piedmont, CA 94611
www.writersadventureguide.com

Printed in the United States of America
First Printing: July 2009

ISBN 978-0-9823442-5-5

Cover Design by Heather Smith, Heatha B Designs
Book Design by Edie Fogel
Edited by Robin Reisberg and Ezra Barany

Barany Publishing books are available for special promotions to organizations and other groups. Please contact us for details.

This book is dedicated to my parents, Robin and Martin Reisberg, without whom I would have never embarked on my writer's adventure.

Contents

Acknowledgments

Every writer stands on the shoulders of those who have gone before. I give a huge acknowledgment to the work of Joseph Campbell, author of *The Hero with a Thousand Faces*, and to Christopher Vogler, author of *The Writer's Journey: Mythic Structure for Writers*. I also give homage to all who wrote down the countless fairy tales and folk tales I've devoured from a very young age. This book grew out of many workshops and talks. I'd like to thank all the students and clients who attended and played with this new material.

A heartfelt thanks goes to Karen Stanwood, Don Kirchner, and friends in Point Roberts, WA, where I presented my workshop for the very first time.

A big thanks to creative colleague Peter J. Ferguson who held my feet to the fire from the first moments this idea was a mere inkling of a passion. A special thanks to Richard Stromer who helped me create my Writer Archetypes. A deep thanks to the women who have midwifed this book in various ways: Edie Fogel, Cara Gardner, Cheryl Liquori, Deborah Le Sueur, Derri Pollack, Robin Reisberg, Jeri Schobe, Heather Smith, Sarah Streicher. I lift a glass of thanks to my inestimable critique partners: Kay Keppler and Patricia Simpson. And this book would not even be here if it were not for the steadfast and unwavering support in so many ways of my husband, Ezra Barany.

Introduction

The Writer's Adventure Guide was designed for writers who want support every step of the way while they write their books. This book will help you keep an eye on your inner landscape so you can fully harness your skills and abilities to go from start to finish on your novel or creative nonfiction book.

The Writer's Adventure Guide has been designed to inspire and motivate first-time book authors who write fiction and creative nonfiction:

- TO FORGE A CLEAR PATH FROM INSPIRATION TO COMPLETION
- TO BUILD CONFIDENCE IN YOUR WRITING INSTINCTS
- TO CREATE MORE TIME AND SPACE TO ENJOY THE BOOK WRITING PROCESS
- TO DELIGHT IN THE CREATIVE ADVENTURE, BOTH ITS UPS AND ITS DOWNS
- TO COMPLETE YOUR NOVEL OR CREATIVE NONFICTION BOOK

HOW *THE WRITER'S ADVENTURE GUIDE* CAME TO BE

We all experience blocks. At times, we all experience a lack of inspiration. Following these twelve stages will allow you to be re-inspired, recommitted and get your book done. With the twelve stages you will improve your productivity, tap into your inspiration much more quickly, come up with ways and tools and your own personalized techniques for overcoming your own writer's block, and get your book finished.

This book was designed for writers who want support every step of the way while they write their books. *The Writer's Adventure Guide* helps you keep an eye on your inner landscape so you can fully harness your skills and abilities to go from start to finish on your novel or creative nonfiction book.

The Writer's Adventure Guide was developed out of my desire to stay in touch with the inner workings of my own writing process. It was not enough for me to learn the craft, I wanted to also acknowledge and work with the inner dimensions of being a writer. I looked for a framework, something big enough to encompass all of my life, but found nothing in other books that spoke to me.

Over the course of writing my second novel, I rediscovered Christopher Vogler's The Writer's Journey: Mythic Structures for Writers, Second Edition, as a guide to writing that book. I was struck by how natural it felt to be applying the Hero's Journey structure to my story, and realized that I had found my internal story structure as a writer.

Later, when I began to help clients, I struggled again to find ways to honor their process, including all the times they resisted writing, procrastinated, or were stuck. While I deeply believe we are all inherently creative, and that with our creativity we can achieve any goal we set our minds to, I was struck by how struggle-free many writers would like the writing process to be.

Creativity can be and has been defined many different ways. The macro view is humbling. In Creativity: Flow and the Psychology of Discovery and Invention, Professor Mikaly Csikszentmihalyi defines creativity as "a process by which a symbolic domain is changed." He states that "creativity does not happen inside people's heads, but in the interaction between a person's thoughts and a sociocultural context. It is a systemic rather than an individual phenomenon."

We write in the context of our times and our culture.

I believe creativity means being resourceful. Creativity is our birthright.

When I set about bridging the gap between our creativity and how that could help writers, I was inspired by the tarot, by images that mark states of being and action. Yet, tarot was not an easily understood progression of steps. Instead, what flowed from my pen, on that sunny afternoon on my patio, was this – the twelve stages of the Hero's Journey as applied to writing.

Finally, I felt I had found a map that encircles all of the joy and tribulations of being a writer. In fact, without really realizing it, I was drawing from fiction tools to help writers gain clarity on what they were writing and why.

Since I learn by doing, I launched classes and workshops, and even an home-study course for do-it-yourself-ers. And thus, the Writer's Adventure was born.

Writing as an Adventure: The Basics

DEFINING THE WRITER'S ADVENTURE

I see our life as an adventure. If we look at everything in our lives through the framework of adventure, then we see that the ups and the downs, the pain, the joy, the sorrow, the anxiety, the frustration, the anger at ourselves and the world are all part of this adventure. That means that nothing exists outside of that adventure, including our writing.

A lot of people call life a journey, but I like to think of life as an adventure, because for me, adventures are fun. So is creativity, and so is writing books.

I welcome you to this Writer's Adventure.

FUN = JOY = PLAY = CHALLENGE = TEST THE LIMITS =
INVENT = CURIOSITY = ADVENTURE

WHO THE WRITER'S ADVENTURE GUIDE IS FOR

The Writer's Adventure Guide is for aspiring authors who are motivated to write their first book. You may want to know exactly how to write the book while living your active life. You may want an experienced guide with you every step of the way.

The Writer's Adventure Guide is also for writers who have already written one or two books, and are stuck. You may be confused and wonder if you are doing things "correctly." You may wonder if there is another way to proceed.

Additionally, *The Writer's Adventure Guide* is for writers who have started many books but never finished one. You may want the experience of actually completing a book.

HOW LONG IT TAKES TO COMPLETE THE WRITER'S ADVENTURE

Many people ask me how long is needed to write a book. I tell them as long as it takes. I tell them gently, of course.

If you follow the steps outlined in this book, the structured answer is that you can complete a first draft in 12 weeks, or three months.

Of course, you can write it in less than twelve weeks. Many people have. I recommend you take the full three months to integrate the material and exercises into your writing life.

Each stage comes with exercises and space to write. Think of this book as your field guide to your personal writing adventure. Crack the spine. Use this book to get down and dirty with the truth of the matter.

While this book was created for book authors specifically, you can apply this material to any creative endeavor. In fact, I encourage you to do so. Since my passion is writing books, I decided to focus the Writer's Adventure on that.

THE SOURCE OF THIS MATERIAL

The Writer's Adventure Guide is based on the twelve stages of the Hero's Journey. The Hero's Journey was formulated by Joseph Campbell in his book *The Hero with the Thousand Faces*. Later, Christopher Vogler adapted this material in his book *The Writer's Journey*, written specifically to support fiction and screenplay writers.

I've adapted this material to the actual writing process, and to the internal creative process of being a writer. By following the twelve stages of the Writer's Adventure, you will write and complete your first book. I invite you to join me for the twelve stages of the Writer's Adventure.

HOW TO USE THIS BOOK

Enter the Preparatory Phase, where you go from Stage 1: Start From Where You Are to Stage 4: It Takes a Village. You will take an inner inventory of who you are as a writer. You will define and outline your book. You will take a preliminary look at who your readers may be. In this Preparation Phase, I invite you to peer deep at all the ways you experience writer's block, and invite you to befriend this part of the writing process. You also will acknowledge and gather your village around you to create a support network.

In the Writing Phase, from Stage 5: Accept the Call to Stage 8: The Challenge, you will explore the particular shape of your commitment to your book, face the challenges of actually writing it, take time to rest and assess, and travel through the last haul of finishing your book.

For the Completion Phase, going from Stage 9: The Reward to Stage 12: The Return with Your Gift, you will be invited to taste the reward: a finished book. Then you will dive into rewriting, transforming your book, so you can be prepared to offer your book as a gift to the greater world.

Stage 0: Prepare to Prepare to Write

Every process contains steps, movement, actions, goals, milestones, and a beginning, middle and end. Every journey also has that moment before starting, where you decide to go or not to go. The Writer's Adventure has that moment, too. I call it the zero stage. The zero stage is really making the decision:

- DO I WANT TO COMMIT TO THIS WRITING PROCESS OR NOT?
- DO I WANT TO TAKE A LOOK AT THE PROCESS OF WRITING A BOOK, OR NOT?

Take a moment to answer these two questions, because I know that writing a book is not for everyone, though many people dream of it. Be honest with yourself, and go for what you truly want. I do recommend, however, that if you dream of writing a book, then go for it.

Use these twelve stages to write your first book. Your first book can be just for you. Fabulous! My first novel was just for my writer's group and me. Writing it was a great experience and when I finally finished it, five years after starting it, I felt so proud of myself. I walked on a cloud for days. Though it took me five years, I did it. Currently, as of this writing, I am working on my fourth novel. Persistence pays.

To go on the Writer's Adventure, you need a few things: proper tools, time, the Writer's Adventure mindset, writing material, and a familiarity with brainstorming techniques.

TOOLS: Computer, notepads, pen & paper, a timer

TIME
What you do with your time makes you who you are.

Allow no interruptions; request privacy from your house companions, be they housemates, spouses, kids, or pets. Do not answer the phone while writing. Turn off your web browser or Internet connection. (You are in charge of that.)

Set aside at least an hour per week to follow this book. Integrate each stage into the writing you're already doing. If you aren't writing yet, and you have been wishing to be writing a book, then use this book and its exercises as your first steps toward writing your book.

Twelve stages = 12 weeks.

Tell your family members, your children, your pets to leave you alone for that one hour you are writing. Sometimes it will be less than an hour. Many of the exercises in this book are done with timed writing.

Time is finite. There are only so many minutes in a day, so many hours in a week—1440 minutes in a day, 178 hours in a week. What you do with your time is what makes you who you are. So decide: I am going to give time to my writing. I am going to sit down and use this one hour for writing—not for TV-watching, not for laundry folding, not for reading a book, reading a magazine, surfing the internet or answering e-mail.

Make this one hour your writing time.

On the note of time, I recommend you get a timer. Go to the kitchen store and get a simple kitchen timer. You can also download free countdown timers online. You can also pay for a fancy countdown timer that you can put on your wall, or for your computer. Many cell phones include timers.

To use your time to write, schedule blocks of writing time into your to-do list. For some of you, this means blocking off time in your agenda, as you would any appointment.

WRITER'S ADVENTURE MINDSET

Come with a spirit of play and experimentation. Come to the Writer's Adventure with passion – the passion you have for writing and for the story you want to tell at this time.

With creativity, there is no failure, only feedback. Be open to putting words on the page, even if they are not the "right" ones. Allow your first drafts to be what they are: rough. And stretch your boundaries beyond what you ever thought possible.

For the duration of working with the Writer's Adventure, you're on an adventure, an exciting activity, an exploration! You do not know exactly where it is going to lead. You can experiment! If you do not like this adventure, you can try some other adventure.

WRITING MATERIAL

You need writing material. Whether you write with pen on pad, pencil on pad, keyboard, computer, AlphaSmart® or some other kind of writing tool, I suggest you get your writing tools ready. Have your writing material near you and have writing utensils everywhere at all times: in your purse, in your car, in your kitchen, in your living room, in your bathroom, and in your bedroom. Anytime you have ideas, jot them in your notebook. I have at least three notebooks of various sizes in my bag. Every room in my house has pens and paper handy, ready for those moments of inspiration. Even my kitchen has a pad on the refrigerator and pen ready.

I also carry three notebooks with me. First, I have an "everything" journal. In this one I give myself permission to write anything and everything. The second journal is for capturing investigative reporting-type questions, and the third notebook is for recording new business ideas.

Experiment

Carry a notebook

Find what works for you

BRAINSTORMING TECHNIQUES

Free writing is writing freely without restriction. Write whatever and however you like. In this book, I often instruct you to free write without time restrictions, and with time limits. Those exercises I call *timed writing*.

INSTRUCTIONS FOR TIMED WRITING EXERCISES

To get the most of timed writing exercises, keep these guidelines in mind.

1. Your only job is to write without stopping.

2. Write from the moment you have set your timer until the timer rings, buzzes or otherwise tells you to stop. In other words, do not stop writing during the session.

3. The point is to write without judgment, allowing your words to be as awful as they are or are not, as awesome and beautiful as they are or are not. In other words, withhold all judgment.

That is Stage Zero. You're curious about what it would take to write a book, or you're ready and committed to do so. You have prepared by gathering your writing tools, by setting aside writing time, by aligning with the Writer's Adventure Mindset, and by familiarizing yourself with brainstorming techniques. You are ready.

Let's begin with *Stage 1: Start From Where You Are*.

Part I. The Preparation Phase

Stage 1: Start From Where You Are

How you define yourself as a writer colors your feelings toward yourself, your projects, your writing, your ambitions, everything. Whether or not you define yourself as a writer makes a difference, too. Is it possible that you would be more committed to the dream of authoring a book if you did think of yourself as a writer? I think Yes, *but I completely allow for a different opinion on this point. To start on the Writer's Adventure you need to take stock of all of you: your strengths and weaknesses as a writer and as a creative person, and how important writing is to you. This chapter invites you to take an inventory of yourself and paint a clear picture. Gain clarity of your daily routines and habits, in action as well as thought. The trick in all of this is to step back and be an observer of your life. Foundational to a meaningful life, including the writer's life, is awareness of self and just noticing, especially appreciating what is.*

WELCOME TO STAGE 1: START FROM WHERE YOU ARE

You are now entering the Preparation Phase, Stages 1 through 4. Stage 1 corresponds to the "Ordinary World" in the "Hero's Journey." In your Writer's Adventure, you need to know who you are as a writer. Self-awareness and self-knowledge is central in the creative process of writing a book, and in any creative process. I invite you to spend some time with Stage 1. As part of this book, I recommend you set aside writing and meditation times.

EXERCISE 1.1: GOALS, MOTIVATIONS, CONFLICTS, AND STRENGTHS (GMCS)

Why is it important to know your goals, your motivations, your challenges, and your strengths? As I mentioned above, it is very important to know who you are and where you are, so you can make decisions about where you want to go.

Inspired by the book, *GMC: Goal, Motivation, Conflict* by Deb Dixon, written for fiction writers to explore their characters, I've adapted her material so the writer can get to know herself and her goals better. You are the main character in your writing life.

In Exercise 1, I ask for your inner world and outer world observations. The inner world refers to your experience: feelings and thoughts independent of what is outside yourself. The outer world refers specifically to a tangible result that another could see, touch, observe.

Use the chart on page 28 to fill in your answers.

GOAL

As a writer, what would you like? Many clients answer the outer world component first, and give statements like "I want to write a memoir," or, "I want to write a mystery novel."

Next, my clients look at the inner world aspect of their goal. This can be described as an experience, like, "I want to feel a sense of fulfillment that I've written a book," or, "I want to prove I can write a book."

There is no right answer to the goal section, or any part of Exercise 1. There is only you being truthful to yourself.

MOTIVATION

What gets you out of bed in the morning? What makes writing so important to you that you would forego something like watching TV to do it? That thing is your *raison d'être*, your reason for being, your motivation.

Inner Motivation examples:
I want to share my gifts (vision, story, etc.) with the world.
My mother will finally love me.
I want to know what I think and feel – to discover myself through writing.

Outer Motivation examples:
I want the recognition authorship brings.
I want to be paid as a writer.
I want a Pulitzer (or the Hugo, Rita, Nebula, etc.).

CONFLICTS

Conflicts, both internal and external, take the form of thoughts, attitudes and habits that get in the way of writing. Conflicts also cover concerns and weaknesses. For example, if you notice that one of your weaknesses is that you have a short attention span, that is great information. If you notice that you can only focus on something for five to seven minutes at a time, then I would recommend that, with that knowledge, you set your timed writing to five to seven minutes. Stretch your capacity just a notch and set the timer for seven minutes. With the knowledge that you have a short attention span, you can build on that and start training yourself to have a longer attention span, specifically by using a timer. Other concerns could be: How will I find the time to write? Where will I write? What if my English is not very eloquent? What if no one wants to read my writing? Knowing what your weaknesses are will allow you to work around them, using your strengths.

One of my weaknesses I noticed is that I had many run-on sentences in my fiction. I didn't realize this until a critique partner pointed it out to me. Later, in my editing process, I am on the lookout for run-on sentences, and I use them only where appropriate.

STRENGHS

Your strengths can include your family, your friends, people who are supportive of you. By knowing your strengths, you'll know, for example, that perhaps you like to write poetry, and that you do not really like to write sentences. Knowing that will help you shape what kind of writing you want to focus on. On this Writer's Adventure, we're going to have challenges. But the goal is something that you want so badly – your book – you're going to go after it no matter what. Knowing what your strengths are is going to help you tremendously on this adventure.

Exercise 1 will also help you clarify your habits. When is your high energy of the day? When is your "prime time"? Like prime time TV, we also have prime-time energy. While writing your book you may have a full-time job. You may have other obligations. As my mentor, Eric Maisel recommends, put writing first. If mornings are when you have that higher energy and you get a lot done, get up a little bit earlier and do some writing. If you notice that late at night you're excited to be creative, well, do some writing then.

Next, locate your aptitude with language. Perhaps you want to write a book, but you feel that your English language skills are not that great. With that knowledge, empower yourself to take some courses to improve your English. Check out the local adult schools or search online to take some grammar courses.

Notice also where your talents are and where your skills are. This is important because if you really love to read one kind of genre, but when you sit down to write it, that type of writing doesn't come easily, notice what you're naturally inclined to write. I wrote my second novel as fast as I could, attempting to create a romance. Instead, what emerged was a wide-ranging urban fantasy adventure story with hints of romance. I learned from that experience that I preferred to write fantasy and science fiction.

Lastly, notice your level of enthusiasm. If you had to decide right now how enthusiastic you are about being a writer, on a scale from one to ten, where one is not at all enthusiastic, and ten is extremely enthusiastic, what is your level of enthusiasm about writing?

	INNER WORLD (FEELINGS, SENSATIONS)	OUTER WORLD (PHYSICAL, CONCRETE)
YOUR GOAL(S) AS A WRITER		
YOUR MOTIVA-TION TO WRITE		
YOUR FEARS, CONCERNS, WORRIES – CONFLICTS, WEAKNESSES TO ACHIEVE YOUR GOAL(S)		
STRENGTHS/ GOOD HABITS/ APTITUDE/ TALENTS/SKILLS/ ENTHUSIASM (1-10)		

WRITE TO REFLECT

Write to reflect on your feelings and thoughts about what it was like to fill out the GMCS worksheet. Draft some notes in the lined space below. Whether it was hard, easy, or somewhere in between, or if you experienced some frustration about it, that is all good information. That is all it is. As Joie Seldon, an Emotion Educator says, "Our emotions are information."

Bless this moment. Each moment is sacred. We are all spiritual beings—we all carry the breath of life in our unique physical bodies. Throughout this book, I will encourage you to get in touch with your own spiritual nature. Allow this moment to be wonderful. You have just recognized that you want to be a writer. You write. You are a writer!

I invite all of you, and in fact I knight all of you. There, you are all writers.

Thank you very much taking the time to look at your goals, motivations, challenges, strengths, talents, skills and aptitudes and habits, and for getting to know yourself better. This is all good information, feedback from yourself to yourself.

_____

_____

_____

_____

EXERCISE 1.2: YOUR VISION OF YOUR FUTURE LIFE

Why is exploring your vision important?

We have a vision of ourselves, of who we're striving to be. That vision pulls us forward and gives us a dream that is something greater than what we are living right now. This dream gives us hope and something to reach for. We all need dreams. To really own, feel and know your dream is very good and wonderful. Write about your vision of yourself ten years from now, paint a scene, give it smells, give it texture, give it feeling. What do you see, what do you hear, who is with you?

Set your timer for twenty minutes. Write about your vision of yourself ten years from now. How do you want to feel? What do you want to be doing? Think of your inner world, and then your outer world. Is writing a part of your life? Are books a part of your life? Is some other creative endeavor a part of your life? Where do you see yourself in ten years? And how does this book fit into the big picture of your life, your greater purpose? State in the present tense: I am, I have, I feel, I write, I do... Use visceral, kinesthetic, and sensorial details (seeing, hearing, smelling, feeling, tasting).

INNER WORLD	OUTER WORLD

*Congratulations. You have now completed Stage 1: Start From
Where You Are.*

STAGE 1: ASSIGNMENTS

During the next week, notice if your goal for yourself, your motivation to write your book, your challenges, or your strengths
have shifted, in view of the fact that now you have brought your
awareness to them. Make note of changes in your journal, on
notepaper, or in your computer, wherever you'd like.

Also, during the week, just notice how the vision that you
have painted for yourself resonates in your daily life, and notice
where the vision is already a part of your life.

Write regularly for at least 20 minutes per sitting.

Start your book, using the starting points as a guide.

STARTING POINTS

Pick one or all, or create your own.

Write a paragraph or more about:

- the goal or purpose of your book
- your motivation to write your book
- your conflicts/concerns in writing your book.
- your strengths, good habits, etc.
- one weakness and ways you can overcome it

A WRITING SPARK TO IGNITE YOUR CREATIVITY

"Zest. Gusto. How rarely one hears these words used. How rarely
do we see people living, or for that matter, creating by [zest and
gusto.] Yet if I were asked to name the most important items in a
writer's make-up, the things that shape his material and rush him

along the road to where he wants to go, I could only warn him to look to his zest, see to his gusto."

-- *Zen and the Art of Writing: Releasing the Creative Genius Within You* by Ray Bradbury

Stage 2: Call To Adventure

Welcome back to the Writer's Adventure.
Hopefully a week has elapsed and you have been focused on Stage 1.
If you have let less or more than a week elapse, that is fine, too.

FIRST STEPS

Take a moment to review your notes from Stage 1: Start from Where you Are and notice whether or not your goals, motivations, strengths, challenges and vision for yourself have shifted. Make a note of any observations in your writer's journal.

Here you are at Stage 2. Welcome. This is the Call to Adventure. In many traditional stories, this stage is called "the spark" or the "inciting incident."

You have given yourself the spark, the inciting incident—you have decided to write a book. Congratulations!

You are still in the preparation phase. In Stage 2: The Call to Adventure, I am inviting you to put down on paper what you want to write, what your main points are, and how you'd like to share your writing. You are being called to write your book. In fact, you are calling to yourself. What exactly are you being called to do? That is what this stage is all about. We are writers, so the way we explore our calling is through writing. Here we go!

Read through the following exercises, then give yourself at least an hour to complete them.

EXERCISE 2.1: DESCRIBE YOUR BOOK

In thirty words or less, state what your book is about. This is a little bit of a challenge, I know. Do it anyway, even if it is scary. What have you got to lose? You do have a lot to gain. Pretend you are telling a friend about your book, but she has to go in two minutes because her plane is about to take off. Unfortunately, most people don't have the time or the inclination to listen for more than a few minutes to us ramble on about our book.

_____

_____

_____

_____

_____

_____

Next, list five to twelve main scenes for your book. The order doesn't matter—just list them as if you were telling a friend, "Well, these are the main events of my book." This is your same friend, who now has 12 seconds before her plane stops boarding and prepares for take-off. If you have more than twelve scenes or sections, that is fine. We're just getting started here. And if you have less than five, you may not have a book. You may have something shorter. What you have to say may fill an article or a pamphlet. That is okay. Write your main points down and we'll decide what form is best for your content later.

1.

2.

3.

4.

5.

6.

7.

8.

9.

10.

11.

12.

EXERCISE 2.2: TIME COMMITMENT

Part of the Call to Adventure is to examine your schedule and see when you can actually be working on your book, as well as on these exercises. What kind of time can you commit to this project now on a daily or weekly basis?

Why is knowing your daily or weekly time commitment important? Because it makes sense to fit writing into your life.

Life does not stop so we can be creative. The earth spins, the laundry needs doing, and we write our books. We're all very busy. Many people put off writing a book because they can't see how they can actually make it happen. I happen to know busy people who work and have children and manage to write books that get published. How do they do this? They write in short increments, like an hour at a time. Setting aside short writing periods works for some people. This may not work for you. Experiment to find out what does.

For this section of the exercise, make a decision and commit to taking action for at least a week. If your planned commitment doesn't work, change it.

Experimentation is the name of this game. Decide if you want to write in fifteen-minute increments, thirty-minute increments, or three-hour increments. As an alternative to time blocks, you can also think about your daily writing goals in terms of words: 100 words at a time, 500 words at a time, 1000 words at a time, etc. I know many established authors who write 500 words a day. That works for them. Other authors write 1000 words, or 3000 words. It all depends on how you would like to approach your writing.

Now, if all this micro goal setting freaks you out, take a moment and write for five minutes in your writer's journal about why and how it freaks you out. Just let the emotions come to the surface and name them, and say hello to them, and allow them just to be.

TIME COMMITMENT AGREEMENT. What kind of time can you commit to this book now? Answer each section. This will help you think about your writing time in different ways.

Daily, I can write _____ (amount of time)
Weekly, I can write _____ (amount of time)
My daily word count is _____
My weekly word count is _____

EXERCISE 2.3: TIMELINE

If you have never written a book before, I suggest you give your-self a minimum of a year to do so. If that just feels too far away, allow yourself to shorten that deadline of, say, six months to finish the first draft. If you are motivated to do so, you can write a first draft in three months. If you have written books before and you want to challenge yourself, give yourself a month, or six weeks.

What is your timeline for this project? To know your timeline, start with the end in mind.

Complete the sentence: "I want to have my book completed by...(specify a date)." _____

Then, complete this phrase:

My book's genre is: _____

EXERCISE 2.4: PRELIMINARY MARKETING RESEARCH

This exercise addresses who your audience is, what problem or pain does your book address, and where in the bookstore you see your book. If you do not know, that is okay, just write your best guess.

Some of you may balk at thinking about marketing and say, "This is way too early to think about marketing. Besides, marketing and sales scare me." If this is you, take a deep breath. And another. Boiled down to its essence, marketing a book is just telling the world about your book in a compelling way—inviting readers to your book. It is like painting a big arrow above your book that says, "Check me out! I'm cool!" Use the chart on page 47 to write your answers.

AUDIENCE

Let's explore who the audience for your book is. Be specific. For example, who would love your young adult fantasy novel? Teenagers, ages 12+, boys and girls; women who read young adult fantasy, ages 20+, avid readers. If you're writing nonfiction—a food-oriented memoir, for example—your audience could be 30+ years, women and men, cooks and chefs, foodies who cook a lot—people like you.

The audience for my book is: _____

_____

_____

A. PROBLEM

If you're writing nonfiction, what problem does your book solve, what need does it meet, what answers does it reveal, or what gap does it fill? All of these are different ways of asking: what pain are you addressing, or what problem are you offering a solution to?

Note: If you want to write your book in 8-12 weeks, use the *Project Timeline Chart* in the Appendix.

FIELDTRIP

Where in the bookstore do you see your book? For this week, I invite you to go on a field trip. Go to the bookstore of your town. If you can, go to a big chain bookstore and go to an independent bookstore. Compare them. And go online. Go to amazon.com, abebooks.com, and other online bookstores. Notice how these bookstores categorize their books. Brick and mortar bookstores offer more specific categories than online bookstores. Online bookstores create broader categories. Make any changes to the question: Where in the bookstore do you see your book?

B. READER EXPECTATIONS

Your audience has certain expectations about the genre you are writing. You need to know the expectations of your genre so that you can meet them, and expand them. Your readers also need to know where to find your book in a store.

What are the readers' expectations for your genre? How do you want your book to be similar to other books, or different from them? Every fiction book published gets labeled by a genre, whether it is literary fiction, mainstream, women's fiction, romance, science fiction, mystery, thriller, horror, etc.

Each genre generally ends in a certain way. In romance, the ending is "happily ever after." In science fiction and fantasy, the world is saved. Or not! Thrillers often end with a life-or-death chase with a time lock, a clock ticking down. In mysteries, we find out at the end who killed the body found at the opening of the book. In literary fiction, the end often captures a mood or flavor of life without any kind of resolution, and leaves some deep question with the reader.

Take a moment to think about how you want your book to end, and that can give you an idea of your genre. Even though you haven't started your book, you can start to think about this. If you do not have an answer because you do not read the kind of books you want to write, then go and read some books in your genre. At the very least, skim them. In today's competitive reader's market, you need to know what authors are writing, mostly because your avid readers do.

How is your book similar, and how is it different from other books? And if you do not know, and you want to write a mystery, and you're not sure, then this is a good indication that you either need to read more mysteries or, maybe you do not want to write a mystery and you're actually writing something else. And that is fine too. All good information.

C. EMOTIONAL IMPACT

State the feeling, the emotional impact, you want to leave the reader with by the time they've reached the end of your book. Why is this important? Think about why you read. I imagine most people read either for information, or for the experience of a pleasurable escape. When we read fiction, we get to experience another life, different characters, different settings, and different problems. When we read nonfiction, we delve into a field perhaps that we do not know a lot about, and we're questing after information. Sometimes, we want to be wowed and inspired when we read nonfiction, as with memoirs or self-help books. Maybe we read nonfiction because we're looking for the answer to some problem. Or maybe we read nonfiction because we're curious and we want to know more—we want to expand our minds.

An example of emotional impact: I want my readers to be in love with the characters they've just spent 300 pages with. I want them to yearn for the next book. I want them to love my characters so much that they just can't wait for the sequel. I envision my readers as raving fans. They're excited and ecstatic about the characters and the world I created. That is what I strive for when I write fiction. That is the emotional feeling that I would like to leave with my fiction readers. With my nonfiction articles and books, depending on the purpose of each item, I want my readers to be motivated to take action. I want them to feel excited, inspired, determined and hopeful.

NOTE TO SELF: WRITERS READ

There are all different reasons why people read. If you're not reading, that makes it hard to be writing. Notice, Writers read. They read everything. They read in the genre in which they write, they read outside their genre. They read in completely different disciplines. Currently I'm writing fantasy, but I read romance, thrillers, and mysteries. And in nonfiction, I read about science, about writing, about rock stars. (That was at the gym.) I read about the state of the world in the newspaper. I read about what is going on in Paris, France, in French, since I enjoy that. I read about sports—I love reading about athletes. Yes, I read a lot.

When I go to a new city, I look at the local paper. I'm curious about how people talk about themselves in the local region. When I'm online I read people's blogs who do completely different things than I do, or maybe something similar but they live somewhere else. I'm always stretching the boundaries of what I give to myself in terms of reading. I also read the back of cereal boxes, the phone book, the dictionary, the free local papers, and the paying local papers.

Allow yourself a broad scope of reading. It can do nothing but help.

D. COMPANION BOOKS

The next question is to name a few other books that are similar to the one you are writing or plan to write. Off the top of your head, go ahead and answer that question. Some of you may be wondering why that question is important. It is a good idea to know where your ideas, your information and your passion fit into the whole conversation, because books are a conversation that we're all having with each other.

For example, when I was working on putting this content into a book, I knew my content was similar to *The Writer's Journey* by Christopher Vogler. Some people have also compared my work to Julia Cameron's *The Artist's Way*. Those two books are companions to mine. Which books are similar to yours? If you do not have a ready answer, if your companion books aren't on your bookshelf already like mine were, that is okay. Take this question with you when you go to the bookstore, or when you search online.

PUBLISHING GOALS

If you do not know your publishing goals for your books, that is okay. Let's explore them here. Today your choices include self-publishing, mainstream publishing, digital publishing, and "Other," because things are always changing. I'll touch upon what I mean by "Other" in a moment.

Do you want to self-publish? If so, once you have written a book, you make sure the book is edited, then laid out. You design a cover or pay a graphic artist to design it for you. You pay a printer, and this printer prints your book. Use the "Steps to Self-Publishing Success" in the Appendix as a guide to, among other things, take care of some of the front matter, like the ISBN, registering your copyright and listing your book in the Library of Congress.

A note about self-publishing: Besides paying for the creation of your book, you also need to handle distribution, marketing, and sales.

1. How do you get your book in the hands of readers?
Either through direct sales or via bookstores, online and brick and mortar. It is a big job, but there are ways around it.
2. How do you tell people about your book if it is just you, and you do not have a marketing department, the way a publisher does?
3. How do you handle sales?

For the self-publisher, there are solutions to each of these questions. In fact, for many kinds of nonfiction, self-publishing is more viable than traditional publishing. If you're interested to learn more, check out the checklist in the Appendix, "Steps to Self-Publishing Success."

What is traditional publishing? There are five major publishers that dominate the publishing industry. See the Appendix for that information. How do you get accepted by traditional publisher? Two ways. One, you could get an agent and your agent pitches to an editor. Or two, you pitch it to an editor directly. This involves a lot of patience and takes a lot of time. Information on querying and how to find agents and editors is also in the Appendix.

Third is digital publishing. By digital, I mean e-books. I have an e-book, *Overcome Writer's Block*, at www.overcomewritersblock. com. It didn't hardly cost me anything to create and put online. One of the pros of e-books is very low cost. One of the cons is letting people know about it, marketing. When I first put it online, I had only 200 people on my mailing list. Now many more people know about it, so there's many more opportunities to purchase. I also use social media and online social networking to get the message out.

Now, what is "Other"? "Other" is hybrid self-publishing. There are publishers out there who will help you in marketing, distribution, publicity, and sales for a fee. They have the infrastructure set up and you pay them to print your book, if they want. Sometimes, there's an approval process because your book has to fit in with some of the other books that they're promoting. But other publishers will gladly take your cash and create a book for you. For a fraction of the cost to self-publish, or maybe for about the same price as self-publishing, but with this added infrastructure, you could get your book out into bookstores. Both hybrid and self-publishing are used predominantly by nonfiction authors who use their book to promote their business.

ALTERNATIVES TO BOOK PUBLISHING

Perhaps you're not ready for a book. There are other ways to publish your material. You can publish through your own blog, or directly on a writer story sharing site, such as www.Novelmaker. com, or www.webook.com. In these sites, you can post your material, maybe get it published, receive feedback.

You can also record your book into audio and distribute it online, called podcasting. There are some authors who've done this, and it's a great way to get it attention. If you believe in your material, and are very happy and excited about what you have created, this may be the right option for you. Authors, Scott Sigler and J.C. Hutchins, released their books through podcasting for free before capturing the attention of traditional publishers.(http://www.scottsigler.com/, http://jchutchins.net/)

There is another way you can publish your work, and that is simply by sharing it with your writing group. For some people this is all they need. I believe that we need to have an audience when we write our work. If we're not sure about the other audiences, or we do not want to take the time, or we're just not ready, having a critique group is a fabulous way to have an audience. You can also share your work with your friends and your family, and they can also be your audience.

1. WHO IS YOUR AUDIENCE(S) FOR THIS BOOK? a. If you're writing nonfiction, what problem does your book solve?	
b. If you're writing fiction, what are your readers' expectations for your genre?	
c. State the feeling, the emotional impact, you want to leave the reader with at the end of your book.	
d. Name a few other books that are similar to the one you want to write.	
2. WHAT ARE YOUR PUBLISHING GOALS?	

EXERCISE 2.5: COVER

Draw or sketch the cover of your book. Why is this important? Visualizing and sketching your cover can get your enthusiasm up. Besides that, it is fun to visualize in a non-verbal, non-left-brain way what your book is about. Think of all the great covers you have seen and just sketch something out. No need to judge your artistic skills. This cover is just for you. Use color if you want. Have fun with it. Be sure that the title is there, and that the author's name is there. It can be your name or a pen name.

Put this cover where you can see it every day. Seeing it there will give validity to the fact that you're writing a book. If you're graphically inclined, create a computer version of your cover and use it as a screensaver or background image. My husband had a lot of fun designing a cover for his still-in-progress novel. You can see it at www.thetorahcodes.com.

Sketch your cover.

EXERCISE 2.6: SYMBOL

Here is another right-brain exercise. Note: In *The Writer's Adventure Guide*, I invite you to do both left-brain writing exercises, and right-brain drawing or sketching. Pick up a colorful pen or pencil, draw in a different color, and just allow your hand to move freely. Just let it move. Notice what you draw.

Draw your symbol.

WRITE TO REFLECT

Take a moment to reflect on what you have drawn. Set your timer for fifteen minutes. Without censoring your thoughts, the images that come to mind, or the feelings that are flowing through you, take fifteen minutes and reflect on your symbol's meaning and how that relates to this writer's adventure and to your book.

_____

_____

_____

_____

_____

_____

_____

_____

_____

Good job. I hope that fifteen-minute writing exercise brought up some new awareness and new ah-ha's for you. And even if it didn't, just notice where your thoughts went and acknowledge and be grateful for this moment.

Congratulations and blessings to this moment—this moment

where you are on the Writer's Adventure.

In Stage 2, I've had you write very specific details about the kind of book you want to write, your genre, what the main points of the book are, who your audience is, the emotions you wanted to leave your audience with, and I invited you to sketch out a cover and to draw a symbol. You have been called to adventure, you are calling yourself to the book writer's adventure. You have sparked yourself to write a book!

Congratulations again. If you still want to write your book, if you truly have been called to write your adventure, join with me next week for Stage 3: Refusal of the Call.

BONUS QUESTION: WHAT I REALLY WANT TO SAY IS...

If you could write a book about anything at all, what would it be about and why? No one is watching, just you, so tell the best truth to yourself, that idea you have never voiced aloud to yourself until now. Go for it!

_____

_____

_____

_____

_____

STAGE 2 ASSIGNMENTS

Check off each one as you go.

1. Fieldtrip: go to a bookstore, a big chain bookstore, independent bookstore; amazon.com, abebooks.com, or your local neighborhood bookstore. Go to any or all and notice how the bookstore categorizes its books. Where would your book sit on the bookshelves? How might it be categorized in an online bookstore?

2. Write in your Writer's Journal about your Call to Adventure. What does being called to your own book adventure mean to you?

3. Write regularly for at least 20 minutes per sitting, either in your journal (see #2) or on your book (see #4).

4. Start writing your book. As a guideline use your notes from the *Exercise 2.1: Describe Your Book* or use the Igniting Sparks below.

IGNITING SPARKS

Pick one or all, or choose your own starting point.

Write a paragraph or more:

- describing your book to someone who doesn't know you or your culture.
- about why there is a need for your book.
- about why you are the best person to write your book.

A WRITING SPARK TO IGNITE YOUR CREATIVITY

Did You Know?

"The product of the creative process is you. ...If you choose to be involved in projects that stretch you creatively, that force you to explore, manipulate, evaluate, and act in challenging ways, then ultimately you will be the beneficiary. And that's the biggest kick of all."

   -- *A Kick in The Seat of The Pants: Using Your Explorer, Artist, Judge & Warrior to be More Creative* by Roger von Oech

Stage 3: Refusal Of The Call

Welcome to Stage 3: Refusal of the Call.

In many traditional stories, this is where the hero decides that he cannot go on the adventure for whatever reason. Conversely, other characters tell the hero why he or she shouldn't go.

In Exercise 3.1, notice why you don't want to write, why you think you can't write, why writing is hard, or why you are not qualified to write. Write about how you are afraid of what might come out if you said what you wanted to say. Notice if there are just too many distractions, or maybe this isn't the right time in your life. Maybe you don't have inspiration to write your book, maybe you don't feel good enough about yourself. Perhaps you don't have a team supporting you, or a mentor guiding you. Write about any and all resistance showing up for you in this moment.

It's very, very important to know what you are resisting, how you are procrastinating, and all the different ways you get in your own way.

Guess what? Resistance and procrastination and all the forms it takes, in other words, writer's block, are actually part of the adventure. This stage is a wonderful opportunity to get to know yourself better, and to find out how you operate, and uncover the triggers that take you off track. Because once you know what they are, you can build positive triggers to get yourself back to your writing.

Appreciate how capable you are at derailing yourself from writing. You are a powerful being.

EXERCISE 3.1: TOP 20 LIST OF YOUR WRITER'S BLOCK

Use this exercise to get your thoughts out quickly. Write as fast as you can. Set your timer for sixty seconds. Good.

Write as fast as you can twenty ways writer's block shows up in your life. You could list people, outer distractions, specific negative self-talk, complaints, a lack of a clear goal, or different forms of procrastination. Be specific, and don't be shy—no one's going to see this, only you. For example, your writer's block could manifest as the laundry, a cluttered desk, the cat, etc.

Timed exercise: 60 seconds

1.

2.

3.

4.

5.

6.

7.

8.

9.

10.

11.

12.

13.

14.

15.

16.

17.

18.

19.

20.

Ding. That was one minute. How did that feel? It's okay if you didn't get all the twenty done, I wanted you to experience also the length of a minute. If you want, go ahead and scribble the rest. Okay, stop. How did it feel? How did it feel to get all of that out of your head and onto the paper?

"If Resistance couldn't be beaten, then there would be no Fifth Symphony, no Romeo and Juliet, no Golden Gate Bridge. Defeating Resistance is like giving birth. It seems absolutely impossible until you remember that women have been pulling it off successfully, with support and without, for fifty million years."

-- From the chapter called "Resistance Can Be Beaten," *The War of Art: Break Through the Block and Win Your Inner Creative Battle* by Steven Pressfield

EXERCISE 3.2: FLIP IT

Reread your List of Twenty exercise.

Take one of your items on your list. Maybe you wrote, "I have no time to write." Flip the item to "I find time to write." Next, write how this new affirmation could manifest in your life. Be specific. Don't worry exactly how this will work, just brainstorm possibilities. For instance, add "I write for 15 minutes during lunch;" or "I write for 10 minutes in the car before going in to the office." In this way, you're opening up the channels in your heart and your mind to create a new reality for yourself, one where writing is a central part of your expression. Take a moment to visualize yourself finding the time to write. You've just rewired a pathway in your brain.

If lack of time is an issue for you, I challenge you to step away from your desk and write in the bathroom for fifteen minutes, if that's the only place you can go. Better yet, if you can, leave the building and sit outside. If it's good weather, do that. Or sit in a different section of the building and write for fifteen minutes. You will notice that you can make progress on your book this way.

Flip another item from your list. Maybe you can't write because you are unfocused. Okay, what's the opposite? Focused. In order to create going from unfocused to focused, you are going to do a short timed writing on your book for three minutes. Because focusing can be difficult, choose a short time span and see how much writing you can actually do. Yeah, there are no good excuses. During the week, spend three minutes per day writing your book—that's all you are going to do. Visualize yourself setting the timer for a short period of time and writing.

Choose another word or phrase to flip. I wrote on my list "angst." I have this free-floating anxiety about my current work in progress. Now, flip it. What's the opposite of angst for me? The first thing that comes to mind is luxury. How can I make my writing time luxurious? How can I create ease? The first thing that comes to mind is a nice chair. Well, I have a nice chair, so I need to make sure that I enjoy being in my chair. This tells me that I need to be physically comfortable when I write, so that's a good awareness for me. When I sit down to write in my designated writing time, I need to feel comfortable, luxurious, and at ease. I will remember to be warm enough, or be cool enough, or to have enough nutrients in my body, and to enjoy and luxuriate in that place of sitting down in my chair and writing.

EXERCISE 3.2: FLIP IT

1. _____

_____

2. _____

_____

3. _____

_____

EXERCISE 3.3: INTERVIEW THE INNER CRITIC

Some of you may think of your inner critic as the wild woman in the basement, the overbearing mother, that second-grade teacher who criticized your writing, or the inner editor who hates a misspelled word. Whoever your inner critic is, it criticizes your writing, your creativity, or even your dreams. It's time to interview him, her, or it.

Start with an initial for your name in my case, "B" for Beth.

> B: Hi, Inner Critic. Who are you?
> Then I'll use "C" for Critic. My critic will write and answer.
> C: I'm the person who wants everything to be perfect.
> Then I'll say:
> B: Great. So tell me, why are you bothering me today?

In your case, maybe you've noticed that, every time you sit down to write, your inner critic tells you that what you write is full of baloney. Ask your inner critic, "Why are you criticizing my writing every time I sit down to write?" Then give room for your inner critic to answer you.

State your boundaries. Ask how your inner critic can help you. It is a part of you and so you need to make friends with it. I firmly believe that these internal voices that we carry around with us serve some purpose. It's your job to be in charge and negotiate terms with your inner critic, so it works for you, and not the other way around. You need to give it a job because it is not going away. Since you cannot "get rid" of the critic, you need to find a job for it that serves you. You can negotiate with it and have it change jobs.

For this exercise, give yourself a minimum of twenty minutes. Set your timer and let yourself interview her, him, or it. Allow yourself to have a real heart to heart. Be honest.

Some other questions that you can ask your inner critic:

When did I first meet you?
When did you first come into my life?
Why are you here?
What do you think your purpose is?

Have fun with this exercise. Repeat as many times as necessary.

Timed exercise: 60 seconds

_____

_____

_____

_____

_____

_____

_____

_____

"Resistance has no strength of its own. Every ounce of juice it possesses comes from us. We feed it power by our fear of it.
Master that fear and we conquer Resistance."

-- From the chapter, "Resistance is Fueled by Fear," *The War of Art: Break Through the Block and Win Your Inner Creative Battle* by Steven Pressfield

STAGE 3 ASSIGNMENTS

Check off each as you go.

1. On a separate piece of paper, in your journal, or on the computer, flip the rest of your List of 20.

2. Continue to interview your inner critic. Either complete the conversation you started here or bring it to the next level.

3. Write. If you are on the fast track, use the Project Timeline Chart in the Appendix to write your book. If you are just getting started on your book, in addition to the other two exercises for Assignments this week, write two to three times at 20 minutes each. As a starting point, use your notes from Exercise 2.1: Describe Your Book, or use the Igniting Sparks below.

IGNITING SPARKS

Pick one or all, or create your own.

• Who benefits the most from you writing your book?

• Who benefits if you do not write your book?

• What is the worst thing that can happen to you if you do write your book?

• What is the worst thing that can happen to you if you don't write your book?

A WRITING SPARK TO IGNITE YOUR CREATIVITY

Today is the First Day

Though resistance may be futile, we all experience it. Just remember that today is the first day of the rest of your life. When you wake up tomorrow, it will also be the first day of the rest of your life. Each day you get to start anew and honor the writer within. Let her emerge. Let her arise, for there is no better time to write than today.

Stage 4: It Takes A Village

Welcome back to the Writer's Adventure.

In this stage of the Writer's Adventure, we examine how certain people around you are supportive of your writing process. Who are those people, and how can you choose to bring more support into your life?

In many tales, movies, folklore, and fiction, this is the stage where the hero or heroine meets with a mentor where they either learn a new skill, or they are reminded of their training, remembering relevant teachings from their mentor. By now you have done Stage 1, examining where you are as a writer, starting from where you are. You've looked at Stage 2, your Call to Adventure, and at Stage 3, examining your resistance to writing. Now we are at Stage 4, looking at how it takes a village to write a book.

Writing is a very lonely business. We sit by ourselves in front of the computer, or with our notebook. We may be in a crowed spot, like a café, or we may be at home. We may have the music on or we may not. People may be around us, or we may be alone.

Writing is a lonely business because it's ultimately between you and the blank page.

Though I am your Writer's Adventure Guide, I cannot write for you. You know the saying, "You can bring a horse to water but you can't make him drink?" I cannot make you write. As you sit in front of the blank page trying to figure out what to say next, thinking about writing but perhaps not yet doing it, the predicament you are facing is between you, your body, your mind, your spirit and your heart. I am not there. Except for that voice in your head that you've internalized from reading this book, that is. As your guide, I can take you through this incredible adventure, but where you put your feet and where, when and how you write— that's all up to you.

I know that if you want this, you can make it happen. I know that we are incredibly creative beings that can create and have what we want. We decide to act all the time. "I'm going to sit here for a few minutes. I'm going to drink that glass of water. I'm going to walk around the block. I'm going to go exercise. I'm going to read now." Those are all choices that you are making or have made, and you can choose to write your book.

As your Writer's Adventure guide, I'm part of your support team; I am part of your village. So are all your other writing teachers, be they in books, a classroom, online or over the phone.

Another way it takes a village is that we need readers. Most of us write because we have something to say and share with the world. The people who read our writing, they're our village and we love them. I like to say that I want raving fans, happy fans, fans who just can't wait for my next book to come out. I want people who search after my information, who want to see everything that I have written, who value and enjoy what I have to share. I want an audience. They are part of my village. And, I am part of the reader's village for many other authors.

Your village is also your support team, and does or will include: editors, agents, publicists, printers, marketers, sales people, bookstores buyers, and all the technical web folks are all the people in our village.

EXERCISE 4.1: ALLIES AND SUPPORT

Of the people who know about your writing, notice who is supportive and who isn't. Who is in your village? Do you have a mate, a life partner, a child, a grandparent, a parent, friends, writing friends, colleagues that are supportive of what you are doing? For the "Allies and Support" exercise, list all of the people and organizations that support you. Be sure to include your writing organizations. I belong to three writing organizations and I'm always investigating and reaching out to new groups of writers to just see how they operate. I also ally myself with other writers and other people in my writing field, as well as people who write other genres. I belong to a small writer's critique group that meets once a month.

I also attend another monthly writer's group about forty people. We shmooze about the business of writing and encourage each other to keep writing. I also belong to a third writer's group, but this one is online. Include your online groups. Just know that there are lots of Yahoo! Groups for writers, blogs for writers, and schools for writers, both online and off. All of these things are part of your support group.

There is one more thing I'd like to touch on about how it takes a village. There are always going to be people who won't like our writing, who don't support our dream, or understand it, and who don't understand why we're wasting our time on something that may not immediately bring in money or put food on the table. Well, the currency here, I have decided, is happiness. Ask those people who are not supporting your happiness, internally at first, then externally, not to be a part of your support team.

What do I mean by "internally"? We allow people who aren't supportive of us to be in our lives. We do—we allow that. You may have heard of "toxic people." There are several tactics and strategies you can use to handle these people. For one, you can stop talking about your dream with them, and you can stop talking about the book you are writing. Because if you put it out there and they beat it down, and this happens all the time, you are responsible for putting it out there in the first place, so they can beat it down. They're not going to change and it's not your job to change them. You can also develop a thick skin. Until you do, though, I suggest you talk about your book to people who are supportive of it, and of the fact that you are sitting down and writing.

That's a decision only you can make.

In this exercise, rate your list of people in terms of support. How unconditionally supportive and honest is their feedback? Rate them from 10 to 1, 10 being unconditionally supportive and honest in their feedback, and 1 being not supportive at all. Also note how often you get together with them.

Who can you enlist to be there for you: once a week, once a month, occasionally?

Timed Writing: 5 minutes, minimum

_____

_____

_____

_____

_____

_____

_____

_____

_____

_____

_____

_____

Tips and Tricks of the Trade

TIP 1: TRACKING

Like any long project, book writing takes place over time. Regular time sitting down with your writing will a book create. I liken writing a book every day to the practice or ritual of habit of brushing your teeth. Such a mundane and important task that we all do (well, most of us, I hope) without question every day. Whether we want to or not.

One of the tools that we can use in support of our writing is tracking. One of my friends and colleagues says, "Winners keep score," attributed to Albert Einstein. Do you want to win at this game of writing your book? If you've read this far, and maybe done the exercises for the first three stages, I'm willing to bet that the answer is "Yes." Great! In order to win, you need to know where you are and where you want to go. Tracking does both.

Use the downloadable tracking sheet from the online Book Bonuses at www.writersadventureguide.com to track when you write. See Image 4.1 for what it looks like. What's important here is that you write regularly, and that you acknowledge that you've done it. Give yourself a pat on the back, or a cheer. Do something to acknowledge you wrote today. Examples include a break in the garden, a stroll with that special someone, a piece of chocolate, or movie and dinner.

Tracking helps you by keeping you accountable. You can't lie with your word count, page count and notes on the days you've written. A spreadsheet like the one I'm recommending validates your progress. If you aren't writing, the tracking sheet doesn't get filled out. And that's the plain fact.

I love tracking. With tracking, you can get as detailed or as general as you want. I love being able to be accountable to myself for my writing. For me, what counts is that I write. Sometimes I give myself small challenges, and play little games, like, "Today I want to try for five hundred words." Sometimes I have made that a thousand words, and sometimes it was three thousand. Sometimes my goals are about the amount of time I spend writing. Today the goal may be 30 minutes. Tomorrow I decide I want to write for an hour. While I run my company, help clients, and write marketing material for business, I have the general goal to write at least 10 hours of fiction per month. My goals fluctuate, depending on my deadlines and depending on how much I want to push myself.

I note the date, the time I started writing, the time I finished writing, and the total time writing. I include any notes like, "Edited Chapter 11." I also have a field for my location, and a field for word count when I started and word count when I ended. Spreadsheet programs can calculate all that for you. I also have a field for the page number I started on and the page number I finished with, so I can acknowledge specifically what I have written on this day. Lastly, I have a total box at the top that totals how many hours and how many days that I have been working on this manuscript. At the top of this tracking sheet are my goals for the current book. You are free to adapt this excel spreadsheet however you like. You may want to download it from the Book Bonuses at www.writersadventureguide.com.

First GOAL: x pages by [date] (starting [date]) [x pages per day or x words per day for x work days] or x words total

[TITLE]: [x] DRAFT											
Date	time in	time out	total	hr	activity	notes	total word count	words added/ subtracted	pages	wrds/pg	Manuscript pages: 250 words/pg is X pages
9/1/06	9:35AM	10:35am	1	1	input notes for Act I		3,412		11	310.18182	13.648
		total	1		hours			0			

By the way, write me at beth@writersadventureguide.com if you have any questions or even suggestions about the material we are covering.

TIP TWO: CAPTURING RANDOM, WAYWARD THOUGHTS AND INSPIRATIONS

Create a paper folder called "random." This folder is for random thoughts and scribbling. I highly, highly recommend this. There you are, cranking up the creativity on your book, and you are writing, and Bam! Out of the blue you get an idea for your day job, or an idea for another book, or for how to do something differently in your household. Maybe something you want to say to your spouse pops into your head. Great! There are several ways to handle these random ideas. Suppressing them, not a good idea. That creates panic. Not fun. Are you going into a panic? Breathe. Getting your thoughts on paper is a good remedy for your panic.

Feeling as if ideas are fighting for your attention? I hear you.

Take a moment to remember who's the boss. You are. And remember what your current writing project is all about. Got that? Okay.

Now here's what you do with your wonderfully sparkling creativity. Write. It. Down. It will take only a few minutes.

I write random thoughts and inspirations in the margin of my journal, so I won't forget them. Somehow, the act of writing keeps them in my mind. If the interrupting idea is a work "to-do," I put it in my agenda right away. I don't spend time so much on how or where it goes, I just put it at the top of that week's page. If you have an idea for another book or another topic that is not the same as the one you are working on, create a folder for it in your computer or have a folder in your filing cabinet that says, "New Story Ideas." I also have a place in my journal where I just write New Story Ideas! and I underline it. It's not so important to me that it gets put somewhere official, just that it gets written down. I have a belief that the story that is calling for you to write itself will be calling the loudest. I probably have at least 100+ story ideas floating out there. But I'm very mindful to choose the idea that is the most exciting to me, the most vibrant and the most juicy to work on in the present moment. If that wonderful idea is meant to be, and you are meant to develop it, and it's a different idea than the one you are working on right now, you know what? It will come back to you. This I believe. I trust in each of our own innate creativity to pick the juiciest idea for the moment, the one that makes us most excited. This is because at this point you are writing this book for you, for no one else but you.

By reflecting on the teachings of Stage 4, by spending some

time thinking about your support team and who's around you, you can then make some decisions. Do you need more people in your support team, or less? Do you need more resources, or less? What specifically do you need to feel supported in your writing? A lot of us writers isolate ourselves. We're creative types. We may have not been used to being a part of a support group. When I first joined the writers' organization, and met with all these other writers, I was overcome by wonder and gratitude. Here was a room full of people, fiction writers like me, and none of us were crazy, although we all chuckled about how the world thinks we are crazy, because we're writers and make up stories for hours upon hours. It is a very unusual kind of task to sit down, be alone, and write. Many people wish for it and never dare it.

By now I hope you understand that being a writer, while lonely, is also a community process. We're a part of a writing community. We're a part of a writing/reading relationship, and we are a part of culture and societies that bring in new ideas and newer information all the time.

We writers are the content creators! We are the creative people behind a lot of the wonderful new ideas, stories and thoughts.

STAGE 4 ASSIGNMENTS

Check off each as you go.

1. Complete and follow up on your Accountability Partners List.
2. Familiarize yourself with the Tracking Sheet, and use it.
Bonus: Email Beth with any questions or concerns regarding this exercise or any other aspect of the course so far. She is your Writers Adventure Guide.
3. Write. This week write 2-4 times for a minimum of 20 minutes

each sitting. If you are on the fast track, continue using the Project Timeline Chart in the Appendix to write your book. If you are just getting started on your book, in addition to the other two Assignments exercises for this week, write two to three times at 20 minutes each. As a starting point, use your notes from the Exercise 2.1: Describe Your Book, or use the Igniting Sparks below.

IGNITING SPARKS
Pick one or all, or choose your own starting point:
- What support do you need most to write your book?
- What do you need to subtract from your life in order to make room for your writing?
- What kind of writer are you and what kind of writer would you like to be? See Exercise 4.2.

EXERCISE 4. 2: WRITER ARCHETYPE
What kind of writer are you and what kind of writer would you like to be? Write to reflect on these questions — Who are you like? Who are you NOT like? Who do you wish to be?
Timed writing: 15 minutes, minimum

WRITER ARCHETYPE	KEYWORDS	INDICATION	SHADOW
1. THE WRITER	Crucible; Creative, Valiant, Intuitive, Lusty	When you are seated in the Writer archetype, you show up for the work, willing to face its challenges with courage and focus.	The Writer only thinks about writing and doesn't write.
2. THE TEACHER	Mentor; Motivational, Spiritual, Balanced	When acting from the Teacher archetype, you model discipline; guide and encourage others to write into their truth and mastery; write to teach; or desire such a writing mentor to enter your life.	The Teacher instructs based on second-hand or fake knowledge and understanding.
3. THE EDITOR	Destroyer; Clear-eyed, Perfectionist, Thick-skinned	The Editor holds the story above the words, so cuts, rearranges and rewrites to serve the story's greater purpose.	The Editor archetype criticizes and attempts to change everything and everyone but his or her writing.
4. THE COMIC	Trickster; Risk-taker, Rejuvenating, Independent	The Comic is not afraid to tell it like it is.	The Comic is a heckler, plagiarizer, and may act like a victim or orphan.
5. THE MASTER COMMUNI-CATOR	Magician; Flexible, Brilliant, Dual, Listening	Also known as the sorcerer, wizard, shaman, or alchemist, the Master Communicator can operate in any communication realm he or she chooses.	The Master Communicator uses his or her talents in a purely self-serving manner, with no regard to the power he or she wields.

6. THE APPRENTICE	Initiate; Studious, Disciplined, Striving	When acting from the Apprentice archetype, you write to practice and learn your art and craft, even though the end result may be only for you or your teacher.	The Apprentice shirks his or her assignments and doesn't honor his or her purpose.
7. THE PARTNER	Collaborator; Mirroring, Sharing, Listening	When you notice the need to get feedback in your writing, especially in the embryonic stages, you are acting on the Partner archetype.	The Partner asks for advice but is never changed by the conversation.
8. THE THINKER	Hermit; Centered, Truth-seeking, Solitary	Also considered the scholar, philosopher, sage, or wise man or woman, when you act from the Thinker archetype, you are willing to write to complete unfinished business from the past, or to deeply examine meaning.	The Thinker avoids being with the self, can't distinguish between self and other, or is stuck in analysis-paralysis.
9. THE BOUNCER	Threshold Guardian; Initiator, Mysterious, Experienced	When you embody the Bouncer archetype, you are crossing into a deeper awareness, where you confront fears, the shadow self, and have the opportunity to distinguish reality from illusion in your writing and creative process.	The Bouncer stays forever on the threshold without advancing, or does advance only to stay in the dark and never learns to trust the heart.

WRITE TO REFLECT

_____

_____

_____

_____

_____

_____

_____

_____

_____

_____

_____

_____

A WRITING SPARK TO IGNITE YOUR CREATIVITY

My writing mentor's are:

Nonfiction books, like *On Writing* by Stephen King, *Bird by Bird* by Anne Lamott, *The Writer's Brainstorming Kit* by Pam McCutcheon and Michael Waite, and many more.

Fiction books, like novels by Elizabeth Moon, Sharon Shinn, Nora Roberts, Anne McCaffery, J.K. Rowling, Richard Bach, Diana L. Paxson, Diane Duane, and many more.

My accountability partners are:

> My writing critique partners: Patricia and Kay.

> My husband, and fellow writer, Ezra.

Thank you!

Part II. The Writing Phase

Stage 5: Accept The Call

Welcome to Stage 5 of the Writer's Adventure, Accept the Call. In this stage you are crossing what is known in this story as the first threshold. In most stories, this is where the hero or heroine actually begins the adventure. We're also entering into the Writing Phase of the Writer's Adventure, Stages 5 through 8. That's right. If you haven't been writing your book yet, I recommend you start now.

Using what you have learned in Stages 1 through 4, you have by now started writing on a regular basis, whether it's once a week or more often, and you have made your commitment to writing your book. There is no going back. You can't undo your decision to write a book—all you can do now is write it. You can stop writing, but you can never say, "I didn't start writing a book." So congratulations for that. I'm excited for you. How about you?

WRITE TO REFLECT

Take 15 minutes to reflect on everything that you have learned in the past four weeks. I hope by now that you are ready to sink your teeth into your writing.

How do you know when you are ready for your next step? What actual steps will you take now? Be specific. For example, specify time, place, word count, page count, support tools or people.

Timed Writing: 15 minutes

_____

_____

_____

_____

_____

_____

_____

_____

REWARD

Reward yourself for every day you sit down to write, whether your writing session is for five minutes or for an hour. I repeat, reward yourself.

How? Some writers I know pour themselves a glass of wine. I play in my garden with my cats, or take a nap. I also give myself the inner acknowledgement for having written. That acknowledgement also acts as a reward for me.

It's very important that you reward yourself for every single step you take, especially if you've never written a book before. If you are coming back to book writing after having had some challenging times with writer's block, it's equally important to validate yourself for the work you do. Brainstorm here. Some things can include: reading a favorite or anticipated book; watching a movie; enjoying a nice meal; going out to a favorite place.

Brainstorm here.

TRACKING

Every time you sit down to work on your book, use the tracking spreadsheet from Stage 4. What matters is that you have shown up for your dream. What matters is that you are showing up to your writing, that you have committed to your book. The best way to show your commitment is through writing. There is no other way. We can think about our book, we can daydream about our book, but it's the sitting down and the writing that shows our commitment. Keep track of when you write and how much you write. And also, if you can, have an accountability buddy at this point in your journey, in your adventure. I highly, highly recommend it.

Every day that you write, freewrite about your creating process. Set the timer for fifteen or twenty minutes, and focus on just freewriting, anything and everything. Gently bring your mind back to your book, where you are in it, what your feelings are, where you are specifically stuck, and where you are having a great time. Use this free-writing as a warm-up to get into your writing when you work on your book. If you've never written a book before, I highly recommend that you write in short, scheduled timed writing sessions. Try for thirty-minute increments, three to five times this first week. If you can only make it two times, that's great, too. The emphasis needs to be on manageable and sustainable writing sessions.

A little story about manageable writing versus the crash and burn method: When I was a teenager, I went on a long hike with a small group of friends. We walked down to the river. That was fun. Then, after playing all day at the river, we hiked back up the mountain. It was a blazing Southern California day. I was hot and felt faint. One of the adults had to carry me part of the way. By the time we got back to our main campsite, I vowed never to go hiking again. Only in hindsight did I realize a few key things that would have made that experience so much better: 1) bring a hat, 2) bring water, and 3) build muscular and cardiovascular endurance by going on shorter hikes before doing such a big one.

Now, because I maintain a steady workout routine, and am prepared when I go out, I can manage a multi-hour hike well. The same applies to writing. Start small and build your endurance.

ACCOUNTABILITY BUDDY

Now let's speak a moment about what an accountability buddy is. Many people use accountability buddies in business, where they call somebody and say, "Hey, today I made five sales calls." What I'm suggesting is at least once a week you have somebody that you can call and say, "Hey, I did my writing sessions this week. I wrote this many times and I got this much done and I feel great about it." This isn't about showing your writing to somebody—that's a writing partner, a critique partner, or a critique group. I'm talking about somebody who's supportive of your writing and will cheer you on. He or she cares about the fact that you are committed to your book. Check in with your accountability buddy at least once a week.

At this stage in which you are committing to action, the most important thing is that you are writing.

Do you notice I keep saying that?

For Stage 5, send me an email inviting me to be your accountability buddy. You could write, "This is my Week Five, and I have written X amount of times this week. I'm so proud of myself."

If you do, I will send you an e-mail back that says "Congratulations!" If you want, throughout the rest of our program here, I will be your accountability buddy.

Who is your accountability buddy? _____

Have an excellent, excellent week here at Stage 5: Accept the Call: Commitment to Writing. I'm proud of you. Happy writing.

STAGE 5 ASSIGNMENTS
Check off each as you go.

1. Report in to your accountability buddy.
2. Celebrate daily and weekly successes.
3. Free write on your writing process each day you write on your book. Timed writing: 15- 20-minutes.
4. Write at your scheduled times in 30 minute increments, only 3-5 times in the first week.
5. Write the book in any order that feels right to you.
6. Email Beth, Subject line: Week 5 of the Writer's Adventure. Tell her about your progress this week.

A WRITING SPARK TO IGNITE YOUR CREATIVITY
My Prayer for You, the Writer

Pour your creativity, life experience, and writing passion into your book. Let it hold for you all your questions, wondering, wanderings and answers about your life.

May your book and your writing bring you much joy through the struggle, much pleasure through the pain of searching for the right word, and much contentment at the end of each writing day.

You have written. You are a writer.

Stage 6: The Adventure Is Real

Welcome back to the Writer's Adventure. You are now at Stage 6: The Adventure is Real: Writing Your Book. The adventure is real, and so are the obstacles. In many traditional tales, this is where the hero meets allies and enemies, and faces escalating challenges. Christopher Vogler in *The Writer's Journey* calls this stage, "Tests, Allies, and Enemies." By now, at Stage 6, I will expect you to have written a little bit each week on your book. At this stage, I encourage you to pick up the pace.

In Stage 6, I encourage you to learn how to write a book by doing it. There is no other way. While that may sound tongue in cheek, Stage 6 highlights that you have fully entered the new land of your book writing adventure.

In the Writer's Adventure, your Tests are your challenges and consist of writing your book. Your Allies should be clear. They are the people who support and aide you. And Enemies? Enemies in this case will be anyone or anything that sabotages, conspires against you, or otherwise seeks to stop you from writing. Even if that someone or something comes from you.

CHALLENGES = TESTS

You will be facing and managing inner and outer challenges that probably will become progressively difficult—things like time, "I don't have enough time," or the fact that your physical space doesn't suit your writing needs. For example, you may find you need a more comfortable room to write in. Another challenge you may face is energy, or lack thereof. You may notice that you're tired, that you don't want to write, yet you've made a commitment to write. At this stage I encourage you to shore up your support team, rally support, and make a commitment to do what it takes to write regularly.

Let's divide challenges into inner challenges, or writing challenges, and external challenges. Your internal challenges may come up because of your resistance.

Writing challenges may entail details like organization, structure, plot, characterization, setting, or craft-oriented problems. The best resolution for these challenges is to learn from more experienced writers. Have a writer around whose brain you can pick. If you don't have access to a live writers' group, I highly recommend you go online for online writers' support. Another way to learn from a more experienced writer is to read his or her book. See the Appendix for a resource list.

External challenges might have to do with people, the space you work in, and also the issue of time. Notice what is the biggest challenge in these external areas, and dedicate this week to addressing it.

RESISTANCE, MY FRIEND OR ENEMY

One of the things that a lot of writers face at this stage, (okay, at every stage) is an overwhelming sense of resistance. Though we addressed Resistance in Stage 3, resistance is something that comes up for published writers, best-selling writers, in fact, most writers at every stage. They face this resistance and know how to deal with it.

How do they deal with it? They don't let resistance and how it shows up—often as procrastination—stop them. They don't let "not wanting to write today" derail their commitment. What they do is they sit down, notice it, and write anyway.

I highly recommend a book at this stage called *The War of Art* by Steven Pressfield. Pressfield's book is a fun, quick read, with wonderful short vignettes on all kinds of topics that address resistance. You may notice that even though you're now committed to your book, one of the biggest enemies at this stage is yourself. Notice where, when, in what circumstances, and how you give yourself excuses for not writing. Notice also how much happier you are that you've made time to write. Read Pressfield's book and get inspired.

EXERCISE 6.1: WRITING YOUR BOOK

This week I want you to do several things. I want you to focus on who your allies are. Really—who are the support people in your life? Also, who are your enemies and what can you do to rid yourself of their influence? And what are some of the other challenges to the book-writing process? I have the utmost faith that we as creative human beings are perfectly capable of solving any issues that come up. Challenges are opportunities, opportunities to grow, opportunities to enrich our lives. Notice what your specific challenges are to the writing, so you can face them head on.

Now that you are actively working on your book, who are your allies?

_____

_____

_____

Who are your enemies? (Dream stealers, nay-sayers, obstacles, challenges)

_____

_____

_____

What are your challenges?

_____

_____

_____

EDITING

I also want to address something at this point that people start getting overly concerned with, and that is editing. This particular Writer's Adventure is writing your first draft. If you've never written a book before, it's important to give yourself permission to write whatever and however, and not be concerned about perfection. My mom taught me that! Once you've written, you can then fix, change, and edit, and completely rearrange your text. To address some of your concerns and put editing and rewriting in perspective, visit Exercise 6.2: Editing vs. Writing vs. Rewriting. Jot down your thoughts about editing, and rewriting. What has been your experience in the past been of editing and rewriting?

For our purposes, I've defined editing as correcting or fixing grammar, punctuation, sentence placement and structure. I totally understand if, during the writing process, changing things around helps you clarify your thinking. Just notice if you get stuck in that editing process. If you're working on the same paragraph for a long time—say, weeks and months—and getting that paragraph right becomes more important than getting the story out, then I would wonder what you are avoiding, especially at this beginning phase. It's more important that you have the experience of writing pages than fixating on a paragraph. Of course, I know there are some people who would beg to differ, and I totally respect that. If that's your process and it's worked for you in the past, go for it. But if you noticed that you're not writing more pages, and every day you're sticking with one paragraph, then I highly recommend letting it go and moving on.

Rewriting is changing the meaning of a word, a sentence, or a paragraph . Rewriting is when you take the scene and write it completely differently, or from another person's point of view, or when you take a thought and totally rewrite it, so it doesn't mean what it did before. That's great, and there's a place for that.

Notice if you're focusing on that type of writing to the detriment of actually writing content. If so, then it's time to let rewriting go and get back to writing your first draft. One strategy to stay on course is to make some notes in brackets: [This needs to be rewritten], then move on. The important thing was you wrote that idea down on paper because once you write down your idea, you now have something to work with. Once you have written a complete first draft, then you can rearrange, rewrite and edit to your heart's content.

EXERCISE 6.2: EDITING VS. WRITING VS. REWRITING

This week, aim to write on your book at least three to five times, of about thirty minutes apiece. More is great. If less is what happens, that's what happens. Just notice that and move on. Adjust your writing schedule as needed. If you have lost your motivation or you can't remember what it is, revisit that from Stage 1. Notice if what you're actually writing is different than what you had planned to write. That's okay. It happens. Writing is deep thinking. Your thoughts on things have evolved. Excellent. Just allow your vision and even your goal to evolve and solidify. That's what writing is helping you do. So have a great week, and I expect to hear from you on achieving your writing goals. Happy writing.

EDITING AND REWRITING	INNER THOUGHTS	OUTER RESULTS
WHAT DO YOU LIKE ABOUT EDITING?		
WHAT DO YOU LIKE ABOUT REWRITING?		
HOW DO THESE TWO ACTIVITIES GET IN THE WAY OF WRITING YOUR FIRST DRAFT? (IF AT ALL)		

STAGE 6 ASSIGNMENTS

Check off each as you go.

1. Report to your Accountability Partner.

2. Work on Exercise 6.1 and 6.2.

3. Continue to log your writing on your Tracking Sheet, and celebrate daily and weekly successes.

4. Free write on your writing process each day you work on your book. Timed writing: 15- 20-minutes.

5. Write. If you're on the fast track, write your book using the Project Timeline Chart in the Appendix. If you are just getting started on your book, in addition to the other exercises for assignment this week, write three to five times at 30 minutes each. As a starting point, use your notes from Exercise 2.1: Describe Your Book, or use the Igniting Sparks below.

6. Continue working on your book in any order that feels right to you.

7. Email Beth, Subject line: Week 6 of the Writer's Adventure. Tell her about your progress this week.

IGNITING SPARKS

Pick one or all, or create your own:

- What feelings or thoughts arise as you reflect on actually writing this book?
- What is the one thing you wish you didn't have to face while writing your book?
- What does that tell you about your hopes and/or fears?
- What can you do to cultivate your writing allies more?

A WRITING SPARK TO IGNITE YOUR CREATIVITY

Writing and rewriting are deep thinking.

Stage 7: Rest And Access

Hi, welcome back! You are now at Stage 7 of the Writer's Adventure. Congratulations for getting this far. I hope you are writing, and enjoying it, because if it's not fun, seriously, why do it? I write because I love writing. I love getting into the world I create in my fiction. I love being able to put my thoughts on paper, to explain, and to inspire. Be sure that this week that you are having fun. You are absolutely, totally enjoying yourself with your book. This book is for you. Yes, later, you'll revise it and make sure other people will find it interesting, if that was your intention. Right now, you are writing for you.

I call Stage 7 Rest and Assess. In many stories, this is the stage in the journey that's been traditionally called "Approach to the Inmost Cave." This means things maybe getting tougher and more challenging. So this week can have a lot of challenges in it. This is also a time in many stories where the hero or the heroine rests for a moment to get ready for the next big stage.

This week, I want you to first fully congratulate yourself for what you have written, really be proud of it—of the fact that you are writing. That is fantastic. Your book is growing. When I was writing my first two novels, I was so excited about the progress I was making that each day I would print out the pages I had written. And every day my stack would get bigger and bigger. Having so much joy in the process, and printing out my first draft pages made it so much more real for me. If you would like the physical evidence that you are writing a book, I recommend you print out your pages after every day that you've written.

This is also a time in which you might begin to notice how challenging it is to write a book. Don't give up. Notice that yes, writing is a ritual, like brushing your teeth. You get better at the practice of sitting down to write on a regular basis. But at first it can be very uncomfortable.

At this point I encourage you to clarify your motivation for writing your book. Take a moment to think about it right now, today.Why are you doing this? Why is it important for you to write this book? If it's nonfiction, maybe you have a message for the world. If it's fiction, maybe you have a story that just wants to get out. Thoroughly understand and honor today's motivation. And make sure it's your motivation, not anybody else's.

EXERCISE 7.1: ASSESS WHAT YOU KNOW AND ACKNOWLEDGE

Note how far you've come and what you've learned. What can you do to acknowledge, appreciate and celebrate your adventure alone and/or with your support team?

We're on week seven, so you've been working for at least six weeks, hopefully, give or take. What can you do to acknowledge, appreciate, and celebrate your writing adventure, with your support team, or alone? It's important to take some time to reflect on this.

15-20 minute free write

_____

_____

_____

_____

_____

_____

_____

_____

_____

_____

EXERCISE 7.2: ASSESS YOUR CHALLENGES

What's easy about writing your book; what's hard? Who can you ask for help and support?

Are you having fun writing your book?
Yes.
No, If not, why not? Because ... And what can you do about that?

10 minute free write here.

EXERCISE 7.3: REST

In what way can you relax more? Be specific.

_____

_____

_____

_____

_____

_____

_____

_____

_____

_____

EXERCISE 7.4: LIST OF 20

As quickly as you can, list the answers to these two questions:

What have you learned about writing since you began this adventure? What do you still wish to know?

Timed exercise: 60 seconds

1.

2.

3.

4.

5.

6.

7.

8.

9.

10.

11.

12.

13.

14.

15.

16.

17.

18.

19.

20.

ASSIGNMENTS

Over the course of this week I recommend that you write at least three to five times, thirty to sixty minutes, and please do check in with me, or your own accountability buddy to report back on your writing success.

I also recommend that you give yourself some journaling time in which you get to play with writing, where you get to just express whatever you want to write about. This is wonderfully liberating and free. You don't need to focus on your book all the time. You can focus on whatever you want. I recommend checking in with your journal at least one to two times.

Thirdly, this week I would love it (and recommend) that you do something fun that has nothing to do with your book. Alternatively, it can be related to your book, but not writing. Whether that means going to a movie or a museum, pick something that you have wanted to do for a while and that can inspire you. I like to go to art galleries and see new visual art. Pick a medium that isn't writing or reading. It can be visual, auditory, or kinesthetic. Really enjoy art as a receiver, as an audience member, as a fan.

Great. So that is Stage 7. I hope you will enjoy yourself this week. Endeavor to make sure writing is fun for you.

> Suggestion: Print out your daily pages as a way to acknowledge your daily process.

STAGE 7 ASSIGNMENTS

Check off each as you go.

1. Do this week's exercises.
2. Report in to your Accountability Partner on your writing accomplishments this week.

3. Continue to log your writing progress on your Tracking Sheet, and celebrate daily and weekly successes.

4. Free write on your writing process each day you work on your book. Timed writing: 15 - 20-minutes.

5. Write on your book. This week, write 3-5 times for a minimum of 30 minutes each sitting.

6. Continue working on your book in any order that feels right to you. As a starting point, use your notes from the Stage 7 exercises, or use the Igniting Sparks from previous stages.

7. Email Beth, Subject line: Stage 7 of the Writer's Adventure Guide. Tell her about your progress this week.

8. Do something fun that has nothing to do with your book.

A WRITING SPARK TO IGNITE YOUR CREATIVITY

As you write your book, nurture and protect your writing. Show it to others only when you are ready.

You are your first audience.

Stage 8: The Challenge

Welcome to Stage Eight. I call this stage The Challenge: Finish the Book. By now you have been working on your book for seven weeks. And whether or not you are near completion, this is a good time to deeply face that which is challenging, or perhaps scary about this process. I believe each of us has within us the strength to overcome any and all obstacles presented in each of our own lives. Otherwise, why would the obstacles be there? Actually, each obstacle is an opportunity. Many times, in stories, this is the part in the journey, in which the hero or the heroine faces the thing he or she is most afraid of. Whether it's the villain, or some inner fear manifested by an external object such as snakes or spiders, or whether it's the moment the hero or heroine reveals themselves completely to the object of their love, this is where the main character faces what he or she fears the most. This is where you get to face that which you fear the most.

For some people, the fear might be the blank page. For others it could be actually the finishing of the book. Perhaps your internal critic still hasn't been tamed. Perhaps there are other outside influences at this moment. Whatever you fear, I invite you to confront it through the following meditation and written exercise. I call what I fear "The Dragon."

You don't have to do this meditation that I am about to present to you. It's entirely up to you. However, I encourage you, and invite you to take a moment to get comfortable in your chair and I will gently lead you through. When you're done, I recommend that you write down what you experienced. Give yourself at least twenty minutes to write it. And when you're done with writing about your meditation, go right into writing your book.

Read the meditation, then do the meditation. You can also record it for easier use.

MEDITATION

Take a moment to get comfortable in your chair. Make sure your feet are flat on the ground. Relax your arms. Relax your neck and shoulders. Relax your torso and your legs. Imagine that you are walking into a dark cave. You're about to meet the dragon. I call it a dragon, however, it could be any creature, any being that you want to face. Ask the dragon its name. Ask the dragon what it wants. What's scary about this dragon? What does it smell like? What do you sense about its size, its emotional state? What does the cave look like? How does the dragon prevent you from moving forward? What can you learn from the dragon? Stay with the dragon and listen to it.

Now, as you leave the cave, thank the dragon. Bless it for this opportunity. Notice your body. Take a deep breath. Wiggle in your chair and allow yourself to open your eyes. Write. Write about your meeting with your dragon.

EXERCISE 8.1: WRITING MEDITATION: FACE THE DRAGON

Take a moment to still the mind. Take a deep breath and pick up the pen. If it helps to get you going, set the timer for 20 minutes and begin writing. Write about facing your greatest obstacle. Walk yourself into a dark cave and write about what you see there, the form this "dragon" takes. Write out your dialogue with it. What does it want from you? What are its demands? What is scary about this challenge? How does it prevent you from moving forward? How and what have you learned from the dragon applies to your current writing challenges?

_____

_____

_____

_____

_____

_____

_____

ASSIGNMENTS

For this week, write three to six times on your book, thirty to sixty minutes apiece. Notice if you have judgments about your writing, and let go of them. Just continue to write. Notice where perhaps you don't trust yourself or your strengths, or the plan you've created for yourself in Stage 1 and Stage 2. Allow yourself to trust the process. Also, take time for your journal writing, (I recommend journal writing at least twice this week) to acknowledge and reinforce how this book fits into the larger purpose of your life. Remember that vision that I asked you to create in Stage 1? It's good to just check in with yourself and see if you are actually still okay with that vision. Remind yourself why you're writing.

Now, work on your book!

STAGE 8 ASSIGNMENTS
Check off each as you go.
   1. Write. Write 3-6 times a week on your book.
   2. Withhold all judgment and write.
   3. Trust yourself, your strengths, and your plan.
   4. Journal entry: Acknowledge and reinforce how this book fits into your larger purpose in life. Revisit your long-term Vision from Stage 1. Does this vision still hold? In what way, if any, has it changed?
   5. Report in to your Accountability Partner(s).
   6. Continue to log your writing on your Tracking Sheet.
   7. Celebrate daily and weekly successes.

A WRITING SPARK TO IGNITE YOUR CREATIVITY

You have within you all you need to face your dragon.

Part III. The Completion Phase

Stage 9: The Reward

Welcome back. We are now at Stage 9 of the Writer's Adventure. You have now entered the Completion Phase, Stages 9 through 12. You did it. If you were following the schedule at the beginning of this adventure, for the eight-week writing schedule, you have a completed first draft. For all of you who haven't have a completed first draft yet, I recommend that you keep writing, and when you are at the finishing point, come back to do the Stage 9 exercises.

This is the point in many traditional stories, movies, and books where the hero or the heroine receives his or her reward. They have either faced the villain and received the reward for the accomplishment of their incredible feat, they have received the love of the person they were wishing to receive it from, or they've discovered the treasure.

Your reward is having completed your book. You are a writer. Not many people can say that they have written a book, and you have done it—a completed first draft. Celebrate. I encourage you to do that this week. Take a rest. Set your manuscript aside. Let it breathe. Take some time this week to do some journal writing about the book, and some fun things, like envisioning how your book will look on the shelf.

EXERCISE 9.1: ENVISION

How will the reader feel when he or she picks up your book? Describe the visceral, kinesthetic feeling of the printed book.

_____

_____

_____

_____

_____

_____

_____

_____

EXERCISE 9.2: CELEBRATE

List some ways that you can celebrate, and pick the one that makes you the most excited, whether its going out to dinner with loved ones, going to a movie, visiting a spa, taking a nice, long hike, buying that beautiful dress, enjoying that slice of cake. Give yourself a moment in time to celebrate what you have created.

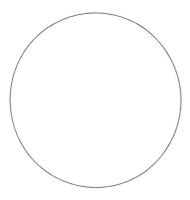

EXERCISE 9.3: APPRECIATE WHAT YOU HAVE DONE

Appreciate what you have you learned from writing your book. List at least ten of the big and small steps, and the big and small changes that you brought into your life by sitting down, writing regularly, and completing a first draft.

1.

2.

3.

4.

5.

6.

7.

8.

9.

10.

EXERCISE 9.4: PREPARE FOR THE ROAD HOME

For those of you who are chomping at the bit to get to the editing and rewriting stage, use this next exercise to list all the things you want to fix in your book. For the rest of you who want to wait until you've taken a break, come back to this exercise later.

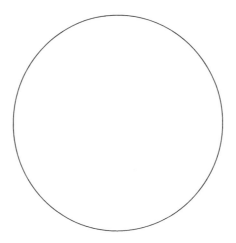

Congratulations. This is awesome. You are awesome.

STAGE 9 ASSIGNMENTS

Check off each as you go.

  1. Stage 9 Exercises:
- Vision your completed book.
- Celebrate your completion.
- Assess what you have learned.
- Prepare for the editing and rewriting stage.

  2. Take a break from writing your book. Let it "breathe."

  3. Share your successes with your accountability partners, including Beth Barany. Subject line: Stage 9 of the Writer's Adventure. Tell her about your progress this week.

A WRITING SPARK TO IGNITE YOUR CREATIVITY

Congratulations!

    You can proudly say that you have written a book!

    Say it! Believe it!

Stage 10: Writing Is Rewriting

Welcome to Stage 10, where writing is rewriting. In many stories, this is the point where the hero or the heroine is on his or her way home, and will probably face challenges that were represented earlier in the adventure. This is the stage where you get to prove book writing to yourself. Stage 10 is the point where you refine your vision, your goals, and what you want to do with your book. Stage 10 asks what kind of commitment you want to make in this final push to finish your book, the Completion Phase.

There are some consequences in writing a book. You can set your manuscript aside and decide, "You know what, that's not what I really wanted to say. That was a great experience, but I really want to write about something else."

I did that with my first book. I finished it, and then I realized that I was not excited to rewrite or edit the book, so I started a new project. When I finished my second novel, I edited it, and then submitted it. The editor didn't get back to me and agent rejections stacked up. I got discouraged about that book, so set about rewriting it, hoping I could resubmit to agent and editors. While I was rewriting the book, I lost my enthusiasm. I lost the fun. So I started a third novel. I continued through many edits and rewrites before I started its sequel. All of that is to share with you that we don't have to stick with this one book. You could decide that it's time to move on to your next book, and come back to this "writing is rewriting" phase on a project that you're absolutely excited about.

Stage 10 is a good time to check in with yourself to decide how much writing, rewriting and editing you want to do on this manuscript. In my world, it's totally okay to decide that it's time to start a new project. In that case, I recommend that you go back to Stage 1 and start a new book. For those of you who are ready to dig in and polish this book up and bring it to the next level because you want to publish it, stick with me and we'll continue with Stage 10.

By the way, there's no wrong way to do things. Whether or not you want to continue editing this book or start a new project is totally your decision. There's only what's right for you right now. Remember, you're writing for yourself.

Take thirty minutes to focus on these exercises to get the maximum reward out of this phase of your writing. Let's look again at editing and rewriting.

As I mentioned in a previous stage, editing is correcting your grammar, punctuation, sentence placement and structure.

Rewriting is changing the content to reflect a new meaning. In rewriting you think deeply on word choice, and use the thesaurus to get more specific language in your writing. For example, instead of describing your character, Mary, as "happy," you choose to describe her as "ecstatic."

In summary, rewriting is about changing your meaning and the sequence of events. Editing is about the mechanics of writing.

EXERCISE 10.1: EDITING VS. REWRITING

Write about what editing is for you and what you like or dislike about it. I draw a distinction between editing and rewriting because they affect the writing in different ways. So notice if you agree with me, and if you don't that's fine, just go ahead and write what your thoughts are about editing. And the same for rewriting—what is rewriting, and what do you like about it and what do you not like about it?

Revisit your notes from Stage 6. And make changes or updates here.

What is editing to you?

What do you like and dislike about it?

What is rewriting to you?

What do you like and dislike about it?

_____

_____

_____

_____

_____

EXERCISE 10.2: REFINE VISION

Refine your vision, emotional and physical goals, and publishing possibilities. Revisit Stages 1 and 2, if you need to. Note what has changed, if anything.

Check in with your vision for your book. Write down your inner world, your thoughts, and your outer world, what outside things might be affecting you.

Let me give you an example. The vision I have for my current novel is of a young woman going through a traumatic and emotional change in her life. My inner vision is about the emotional impact of the story on my reader. The outer vision is I see this book as a paperback, as a mass-market-sized kind of book you see at the airport. I see a book lover reading it and being involved in it. This vision hasn't changed since it came to me a few years ago.

I love the editing and the rewriting process. To me, this is the point in which you get to refine your vision and keep your readers in mind while you edit and rewrite. Say you've decided that your market is 20- to 65-year-old women who read five books a month, mostly romances. As you are editing and rewriting, keep their genre expectations in mind, and work to meet them in your unique and satisfying way.

Review your goals for the book, what your genre is, and what publishing steps you need to take for your book. This will orient you and help you stay clear on the editing and rewriting phase.

	INNER: EMOTIONAL IMPACT ON THE READER/WRITER	OUTER: FORM OF THE BOOK, USE OF THE BOOK; ACTIONS TO TAKE
VISION		
GOAL		
MARKET (GENRE)		
PUBLISH-ING STEPS		

HOW TO EDIT AND REWRITE

How do you go about editing and rewriting your book? See the Appendix for specific books on editing and rewriting. How you go about editing and rewriting depends on what kind of person you are. Do you like to approach projects logically, in a linear fashion, or emotionally? Do you want to move through your book chronologically, or thematically in the rewriting phase? Personally, I need to move from beginning to end. I'm primarily a linear thinker. I simply don't feel that I can jump around when I write fiction because I want things to build on each other, and move from start to finish.

I propose several ways to edit and rewrite. Absorb these processes, then throw them out and find what works for you.

First Read-Through

I recommend that you start by reading your entire manuscript without a pencil in your hand. Print out your book, sit down and read it. Read it as someone else, as an eager reader. See if you enjoy your book. I hope you do. Yes, you might cringe at moments. You might notice where things are unclear and you will also notice where things are clear. You may also revel in the story and lose yourself in the tale you've woven.

Second Read-Through

In your second read-through, you can either do it on your computer or on your printout. Use highlighters to mark what you like and what needs fixing.

Use a yellow highlighter and mark a smiley face next to what you like. Use a green highlighter for the areas that don't work for you.

Note: You can use different colors than the one I suggest. You can do whatever works for you.

If you're inspired, make a few notes about what you'd like to fix, but don't fix it just yet. Continue to do that throughout the whole manuscript.

Third Read-Through

After one day or two, read your manuscript for a specific focus. For example, examine tense and make sure it's consistent. Another focus could be person. Are you consistently writing in the first-, second-, or third person?

If you are not sure where to begin in your editing, go back to the notes you made during the second read-through. Certain aspects of your writing showed up as needing work. What were they?

If you didn't make notes, now is the time. List all the things that you want to edit or rewrite. Start with a short list, written quickly. List things like, "my tenses aren't consistent," "my thoughts jump a little bit too much," "I'm lacking some transitions," "I need to flesh out my scenes," or "I need to add more visceral descriptions." Just notice the overall trends in your editing. For Exercise 10.4: Scheduling, decide what you want to edit or rewrite first, and schedule that out.

Depending on how you like to proceed, you can address editing in a very emotional way, not following any of the guidelines in the books that I've recommended or, you can follow guidelines, and approach editing in a much more linear fashion. I recommend that you give yourself editing tasks in little chunks, thirty to forty minute chunks of editing and rewriting time. This is highly concentrated mental work. You're diving in now and asking the hard questions: "Is this clear? Is this compelling? Will my audience understand what I'm trying to say?"

Enjoy this work, and notice if it's hard or challenging, or easy and effortless. Also journal about that. Keep up with your journaling, at least one to two times a week. Note why editing is difficult, if it is. Editing is what makes writing challenging. It's also what makes writing work, and what makes writing so rewarding. Enjoy this process, and notice that you are writing.

One last thing about finishing Stage 10. Continue to check in with your accountability buddies. If that's me, send me an e-mail letting me know how many times you sat down to edit. Have a great week, and I'll check in with you next week.

LIST 10.1: EDITING AND REWRITING OPTIONS
Grammar
Tense
Word choice
Voice
Pacing
Transitions
Add more sensory details
Show, don't tell
Characterization
Plot clarification
Clarify your story purpose

EXERCISE 10.3: STEPS TO EDITING AND REWRITING

1. Print out your book and read it without a pen or pencil. Your first read-through.

2. On a second read-through, notate general reactions on things you like and don't like.

3. As you read through a third time, pick the items to work on and list them.

4. Schedule time to rewrite and/or edit.

EXERCISE 10.4: SCHEDULING

Take a look at scheduling. Just like you scheduled time for your writing, you're now going to schedule your editing time. Set aside time to edit and rewrite your book and schedule it in your calendar. Also, track your progress on your tracking spreadsheets.

First, choose what to edit or rewrite. Write that here: _____

_____

By Date: _____

Second, choose what to edit or rewrite next: _____

_____

By Date: _____

Third, choose what to edit or rewrite next: _____

_____

By Date: _____

Fourth, choose what to edit or rewrite next: _____

_____

By Date: _____

Fifth, choose what to edit or rewrite next: _____

_____

By Date: _____

STAGE 10 ASSIGNMENTS

Check off each as you go.

1. Edit and/or rewrite: 3-6 times a week.

2. Report in to your Accountability Partner.

3. Work on Stage 10 exercises.

4. Continue to log your writing and editing time on your Tracking Sheet.

5. Celebrate daily and weekly successes.

6. Free write on your editing and rewriting process each day you work on your book.

7. Email Beth, Subject line: Stage 10 of the Writer's Adventure. Tell her about your progress this week.

A WRITING SPARK TO IGNITE YOUR CREATIVITY

Editing and rewriting are re-visioning and clarifying and deepening and enlivening your writing.

Stage 11: Transforming Your Book

Welcome to Stage 11: Transforming Your Book. You're deep in the finishing phase. In stories and movies, this is often called "the resurrection phase." This is where the hero and heroine faces that which is the most difficult, and surmounts it, or doesn't.

How does this apply to writing? This is where you are building your book into something that you can share with the world, whether that's your writing group, your small group of friends and family, online for yourself, self-published, mainstream published, or some other form of publication. You are not done yet—editing takes time. I realize that in the time that we're together, you may not finish editing or rewriting your book. That's okay. It could take many more weeks. but I will invite you to experiment with the idea of finishing your book in the next stage. In Stage 11, you are invited to focus on word choice and grammar. Continue with your editing and rewriting. Notice where it's challenging. Dig deep within yourself to find the motivation to continue. You may notice some challenging moments. You may notice that it is no fun at all.

EXERCISE 11.1: FACE THE DRAGON AGAIN

Take time to face your dragon again. Enter into a meditative state, relaxing your entire body. Take a moment and still the mind. Take a deep breath. Imagine you are walking into that dark cave you visited in Stage 8. See the dragon. This dragon may not be the same one you faced a few weeks ago. It may be completely different. Notice what this dragon wants from you. Ask it. What are its demands? What is its challenge? In what way does this dragon prevent you from moving forward? And what can you learn right now from it? How can you apply that learning to the current challenges you're facing in writing your book? Notice if the information is different from your previous encounter, notice where it might be the same.

You are almost done with polishing your first draft, but something may stop you from finishing. What is it? What does it feel like, smell like, taste like, sense like? What can you learn from facing this congested point? Name the lesson or understanding.

Take a deep breath. Notice if you are in the body, and then return to it, if needed. Pick up your pen or go to the keyboard. Set the timer for twenty minutes and write about what you discovered.

_____

_____

_____

_____

_____

_____

_____

_____

_____

_____

_____

_____

_____

_____

_____

EXERCISE 11.2: QUIET THE MIND AND VISION

As you did in Stage 8, take a moment to still the mind. Take a
deep breath and pick up the pen. Set the timer for 20 minutes and
write about facing your greatest obstacle. Walk yourself into a
dark cave and write about what you see there. What form does
this "dragon" take? Write out your dialogue with it. What does
it want from you? What are its demands? What is scary about
this challenge? How does this dragon prevent you from moving
forward? How can what you learn from the dragon apply to your
current writing challenges? Has anything changed from the previous encounter? What's different? What's the same?

_____

_____

_____

_____

_____

_____

_____

_____

EXERCISE 11.3: EVALUATE

Was this project worth it? Are you sure? Did you say what you wanted to say? Yes? Great! No? Restart? New book?

_____

_____

_____

_____

_____

_____

_____

_____

_____

_____

_____

What was your motivation for writing this book? Check in with yourself. In what way is your motivation the same or different?

_____

_____

_____

_____

_____

You have faced your dragon again. You have learned from it. You're editing. You are rewriting. Continue to do so this week. Continue to put in your editing or rewriting time, three to six times a week, thirty to sixty minutes, at least. Of course, do more if you want. Continue to check in with your accountability buddies. If that's me, write in and tell me that you have written, when, how much, and what.

Know that you are doing the hard work of writing. And enjoying it. Yes, you must enjoy this part of the writing process. The heart and soul of good writing is rewriting. Don't be afraid to rewrite your work, one, two, five, ten times. You are uncovering and discovering what you are really trying to say.

Notice whether or not you are saying what you intended to say and keep trying on words until you've uncovered what you really choose to say.

I liken writing to movie making. It helps me think about my book in more flexible ways, and to move forward with writing when I'm stuck. Every time you rewrite something, save it as a new draft and consider it a new "take," like Take 1, Take 2, Take 3. You are uncovering the truth within yourself of what you are trying to say.

So have a fabulous week with your writing and join me here again next week for Stage 12.

Happy writing and rewriting!

STAGE 11 ASSIGNMENTS
Check off each as you go.
1. Edit and / or rewrite. 3-6 times a week, 30-60 minutes.
2. Report in to your Accountability Partner.
3. Work on Stage 11 exercises.
4. Continue to log your writing and editing time on your Tracking Sheet.
5. Celebrate daily and weekly successes.
6. Free write on your editing and rewriting process each day you work on your book.
7. Email Beth, Subject line: Stage 11 of the Writer's Adventure. Tell her about your progress this week.

A WRITING SPARK TO IGNITE YOUR CREATIVITY
As long as you show up for your writing, you cannot fail.

Stage 12: The Return With Your Gift

Welcome to Stage 12 of the Writer's Adventure.

Yes, you have reached Stage 12. Congratulations. You have a polished book. In many stories, this is where the hero or the heroine returns to their community with a gift. In this case, the gift is your completed book. Celebrate. Really enjoy this moment.

Celebrate!

In Stage 12, you will also look at your publication next steps. Do you need to write a query letter? Do you need to research appropriate agents and editors? Do you need to research self-publishing or online publications, blogs, or e-books?

As you are preparing to sell your book, or turn it into another form, a published form, it is totally okay to start a new book. Notice, though, if your attention and writing time can be divided between two projects. Notice if, on one day, you want to focus on how to publish your book, and on another day if you might want to start a new book.

EXERCISE 12.1: CELEBRATE

In the exercise, Celebrate, write about how you're going to celebrate what you've learned in this process. How can you really thank the group of people who supported you? What is life like now that you have written your book? You may wish for people to treat you differently, or see you in a new light. Has that changed? How do you feel about yourself? Do you feel more accomplished? Do you feel like you have done something quite wonderful? I hope you do. Writing a book is a big endeavor and you've done it. Like I said in Stage 9, not many people can say that they have written a book. And guess what? You have.

How do you celebrate your newfound understanding? _____

_____

_____

_____

_____

How does the community celebrate you? _____

_____

_____

_____

_____

_____

How will you celebrate with your support team?

How can you thank them? _____

_____

_____

_____

_____

How do you reintegrate back into your old or new community? _____

_____

_____

How do you feel about yourself? _____

_____

_____

_____

_____

_____

EXERCISE 12.2: NEXT STEPS AND NEW CHOICES: PUBLISHING CONSIDERATIONS

Begin again on a new journey: to publish, self-publish or start a new book. What are your options? What is your purpose? Try each one on for size. To research the market, and study the pros and cons, to help determine which publishing option is right for you, review the Bibliography for publishing resources and the Publishing Options Report, both in the Appendix and digitally in "Book Bonuses" on www.writersadventureguide.com.

	TRADITIONAL PUBLISHING	SELF-PUBLISHING
PROS		
CONS		
QUESTIONS		
NEXT STEPS		

EXERCISE 12.3: ORGANIZE YOUR TIME

Researching the market? Or starting a new book?

DAY	ACTIVITY
MON	
TUES	
WED	
THURS	
FRI	
SAT	
SUN	

EXERCISE 12.4: SUPPORT

What do you need to do next, or ask for next, to be supported in your next steps?

_____

_____

_____

_____

_____

This week, spend your writing time on one of several things: researching the marketplace, writing a query, or what kind of agents and editors are out there. And if you are so inspired, start brainstorming a new book. You may be so excited about having completed one manuscript that you're ready to start another. In that case, I recommend that you go back to Stage 1 and start the process all over again.

Continue with your journal writing. Journal about your process, about how you may feel complete with writing this manuscript, about your thoughts, worries, or concerns about publication. Also recognize and congratulate yourself for all the hard work that you've put into this process. Check in with yourself. Did you have a good time? Is this something that you want to continue doing? For some people, writing a book is an experiment they don't know if they're going to repeat. Other people will always be working on a book. It may give you immense pleasure—as it does me—to always be working on a fiction book.

Welcome to the life of a writer. You are a writer. Enjoy it. Look! You have completed a book! And again—congratulations! I invite you to keep writing, and to find ways to publish your book. I will have a new series coming out about the whole publishing phase. Meanwhile, please enjoy all the resources in the book, as well as at the website www.writersadventureguide.com, "Book Bonuses." I'm always interested in hearing from you and hope that you write. Write me about your success, tell me where I can find your book, and share your writing life with me. You can also visit my blog at www.writersfunzone.com/blog and share your writing tips with the world. I am always happy to have guest contributors. Thank you so much for joining me on the Writer's Adventure.

STAGE 12 ASSIGNMENTS

Check off each as you go.

1. Edit and/or rewrite, or research the market at least 3-6 times a week, 30-60 minutes.

2. Work on Stage 12 exercises.

3. Continue to log your writing and editing time on your Tracking Sheet, as needed.

4. Free write on your editing and rewriting process each day you work on your book, as needed.

5. Email Beth, Subject line: Stage 12 of the Writer's Adventure. Tell her about your success. And stay in touch! You're invited to

query Beth to write a "how to" piece for her blog, the Writer's
Fun Zone, http://www.writersfunzone.com/blog.

A WRITING SPARK TO IGNITE YOUR CREATIVITY

Welcome to the life of a writer! Congratulations!

May the adventure begin again!

Appendix

First GOAL: Complete a 250-page book in 12 weeks; Write actively for 8 weeks				
[Your TITLE]: First Draft				
Week	Words to write per day (5 days per week)	total word count	pages	words per page
Week 1				
Week 2				
Week 3				
Week 4				
Week 5	1600	8000	32	250
Week 6	1600	8000	32	250
Week 7	1600	8000	32	250
Week 8	1600	8000	32	250
Week 9	1600	8000	32	250
Week 10	1600	8000	32	250
Week 11	1600	8000	32	250
Week 12	1600	8000	32	250
		64,000	*256*	
		words	*pages*	
		total		

First GOAL: Complete a 250-page book in 12 weeks; Write actively for 12 weeks				
[Your TITLE]: First Draft				
Week	Words to write per day (5 days per week)	total word count	pages	words per page
Week 1	1100	5,500	22	250
Week 2	1100	5,500	22	250
Week 3	1100	5,500	22	250
Week 4	1100	5,500	22	250
Week 5	1100	5,500	22	250
Week 6	1100	5,500	22	250
Week 7	1100	5,500	22	250
Week 8	1100	5,500	22	250
Week 9	1100	5,500	22	250
Week 10	1100	5,500	22	250
Week 11	1100	5,500	22	250
Week 12	1100	5,500	22	250
		66,000	*264*	
		words	*pages*	
		total		

STEPS TO SELF-PUBLISHING SUCCESS

#	STEPS TO PUBLISH A BOOK	TIME COMMITMENT
1	1a. Writing & Research, plus Planning 1b. Book Creation Planning 1c. Book Marketing Planning	1 week
2	Editing	1-2 weeks
3	Copy editing	1 – 3 days
4	Proofreading	1 day
5	ISBN (and front matter)	1 day
6	Cover art (Once you have a cover and a web presence, start marketing your book.)	1 week
7	Book layout and design	1-2 weeks
8	Printing Set-up Fee for POD	1-2 weeks
9	Get busy marketing your book according to your plan	ongoing

1A. WRITING & RESEARCH

Determine how many hours a day you can work on your book. Commit to that time and tell your coach. Decide how much of that time will be for writing and research, and how much of that time will be planning and executing on book creation and book marketing.

Many writers set daily goals, either pages or word count. Many writers write about 500-1000 words an hour, or 2-4 pages per hour. Many writers set aside at least an hour a day for planning and marketing.

Beside staying accountable to your coach, what kind of reward will you give to yourself by writing daily? Rewards can be a thing or an experience you give yourself.

1B. BOOK CREATION PLANNING
1. Determine a book title and subtitle.
2. Fill the Book Marketing Planning Sheet.
4. Determine how to distribute and sell your book.
5. Determine book size.
6. Determine which print-on-demand company to go with. Do price and time comparisons. If you decide to go with LSI, read on.
7. Hire a graphic artist for the cover; give artist 3 examples from existing books of what you'd like (colors, font, look & feel).
8. Upon completion of manuscript, hire an editor.
9. Hire a book designer to layout book.
10. Set up your book with LSI.
11. Submit completed book to LSI.

1C. BOOK MARKETING PLANNING

Author's Name:	Estimated Publication Date:
Title:	Price:
Sub-Title:	ISBN:
Genre:	Estimated Marketing Budget:

POSITIONING

Target Audience

Describe your target audience. Include demographics and psychographics. Determine the size of your target audience.

Marketability

Where does your target audience gather? Online and in-person? What do they read? How will you get this book into their hearts and minds?

Author

What qualifies you to write this book? How are you the expert? What's your "angle"?

Problem/Solution

What problem(s) or condition(s) does your book address or solve? Be specific.

Benefits

What are the deep benefits your reader experiences from reading your book? Name at least 2.

Competition

Name 5-20 other book titles that are similar. Determine what makes your book different and similar. Use the "Other people bought..." feature on amazon.com to research your competition. Go to bookstores, too.

Selling Points

What are three unique selling points about your book that

distinguish it from similar books?

1.

2.

3.

AUTHOR PLATFORM & PROMOTION
Target size of email database:
Target size of mailing list:
Web/Blog URL:_____

LIST OF POSSIBLE PROMOTIONAL STRATEGIES:
Be specific. For example, using Twitter, Facebook, speaking engagements, an amazon.com best-seller campaign, etc.

NEXT STEPS
For STEPS 2-4 AND 6-7 please check in with your coach for referrals and support.

5. ISBN AND FRONT MATTER
Check off each item as you go.

____ Get your own ISBN number from RR Bowker. One ISBN ($99) and a FREE EAN barcode can be obtained from this address: https://isbn.selfpublishing.com/application.php or buy 10 ISBN numbers for $245 at: http://www.isbn.org/standards/home/isbn/us/secureapp.asp

"If you have not obtained your ISBN number (actually ten are the minimum) from RR Bowker, you do not own it. Buying your own ISBN is the single most important thing that you will do as an Independent Publisher... The ISBN number is what identifies you as the publisher. Once you have obtained your ISBN numbers from RR Bowker, you are no longer a 'self-publisher' you are 'A' publisher - an Independent Publisher. There is no difference at that point between you and Random House except for the fact that Random House publishes more titles than you (more than most publishers for that matter). You assign one of these numbers to your first book. Once you own the ISBN number, it remains the same for the life of the book. You can change printers, distributors, wholesalers or retailers. You can change whatever you want. The book remains yours. If ten years from now, someone orders a copy of your book, you, as the publisher, will get the order. If you don't own the number, the person who does, will get the order. Most of these vanity/subsidy presses will not even be around ten years from now so the order for that book will end up going unfulfilled."

  -- http://splash.selfpublishing.com/question5.php

_____ Once you have an ISBN number, register at Bowkerlink Online to be listed in Books in Print: www.bowkerlink.com
 -- FREE

_____ Request a Library of Congress number. For self-publishers it is called a PCN: pcn.loc.gov -- FREE

_____ Get a BISAC code for FREE at the BISG site: www.bisg.org

_____ Apply for a SAN (Standard Address Number) at www.isbn.org -- FREE

RESOURCES

Small Publishers Association of North America: spannet.org

Independent Book Publishers Association:
http://www.pma-online.org/

Bay Area Independent Book Publishers Association:
http://www.baipa.net/

Traditional Publishing

THE OBJECT OF THE GAME IS: GET PUBLISHED!
Know the rules...

REALITY
(As of Dec. 2006)

PUBLISHERS
Five multinational corporations own most of the mainstream publishers in the US.

1. Bertlesmann AG owns Random House, including such imprints as the Bantam Dell Publishing Group.

2. CBS Corporation owns Simon & Schuster, Pocket Books, and other imprints.

3. Disney owns Hyperion.

4. Lagardère owns the TimeWarner Book Group which includes Warner, Little, Brown and Company and all their subdivisions.

5. Rupert Murdoch's News Corp. owns HarperCollins and its many imprints.

In the US and Canada there are hundreds of independent publishers, including university presses.

AGENTS

Agents come in two varieties: AAR-approved and not AAR-approved.

AAR: www.aar-online.org/ Membership to the Association of Authors' Representatives means agreeing to their Canon of Ethics.

PUBLICATION CYCLE

Overnight success is mostly not real.
Your timeline is no one else's.

DEFINE YOUR FICTION TO SELL IT

Sell your book to an agent who sells it to an editor who sells it to the other editors on the team (so everyone is on board) who sell it to the sales force who sell it to the book distributor who sells it to the booksellers who sell it to the assistant booksellers who sell it to the readers.

"ELEVATOR PITCH"

Practice. Rehearse. Repeat.

ELEVATOR PITCH FORMULA

SITUATION: (Also called the Initial Action or Premise, this is the beginning of the plot.)
MAIN CHARACTER(s): (Self-explanatory)
PRIMARY OBJECTIVE: (At first, what does your main character want?)
ANTAGONIST OR OPPONENT: (or Central Conflict. Who or

what is keeping your main characters from getting what they want?)

DISASTER THAT COULD HAPPEN: (What's the worst that could happen, and/or what does your character want next? Often phrased as a question.)

EXAMPLE 1:
Initial Situation: Married to the young girl's mother,
Main Character: Humbert Humbert
Primary Objective: lusts after his nymphet stepdaughter, Lolita,
Antagonist or Opponent: but giving in to his pedophilic fantasies
Disaster That Could Happen: would destroy his seemingly normal life he has carefully forged.

EXAMPLE 2:
Initial Situation: Abandoned on his relatives' doorstep as an infant,
Main Character: Harry Potter
Primary Objective: longs to understand where he came from and why he feels different.
Antagonist or Opponent: He discovers that he is a wizard and that his parents were killed by Voldemort, a powerful and evil wizard,
Disaster That Could Happen: who has been hunting for Harry, to kill him.

EXAMPLE 3:
Initial Situation: When his father dies unexpectedly,
Main Character: Hamlet, the prince of Denmark,

Primary Objective: is away and cannot claim the throne, and then discovers that his father may have been assassinated by . . .
Antagonist or Opponent: His uncle, who was elected king of the semi-democratic monarchy,
Disaster That Could Happen: and who now may be trying to kill Hamlet.

Adapted from http://www.fundsforwriters.com/elevatorpitch.htm

Other great examples and query tidbits:
Fiction:: http://peggypayne.blogspot.com/2005/12/elevator-pitch-for-selling-your-art.html

Nonfiction:: http://writingshow.com/?page_id=4

QUERY LETTER
Form and content. Rewrite until it shines. A request to get your material read. Site: www.agentquery.com/ has many examples.

Some Tips and Tricks To Get Noticed
1) Write your best book, and have it completed before you query.
2) Network at writers associations and get a published author to recommend you to their agent.
3) Network and pitch to agents and editors at conferences, then follow up with a cover letter, synopsis, and requested pages.

WRITERS ASSOCIATIONS

Romance Writers of America (RWA) -- www.rwanational.org

Mystery Writers Association -- www.mysterywriters.org/

Sisters in Crime -- www.sistersincrime.org/

Science Fiction & Fantasy Writers of America, Inc. -- www.sfwa.org/

California Writers Club -- www.calwriters.org/ (local yearly conference)

Broad Universe -- www.broaduniverse.org/

National Writers Union -- www.nwu.org/

Horror Writers of America -- www.horror.org/

The Authors Guild -- www.authorsguild.org

International Thriller Writers, Inc. -- www.thrillerwriters.org/

Society for Children's Book Writers & Illustrators -- http://www.scbwi.org/

American Christian Fiction Writers -- http://www.americanchristianfictionwriters.com/

CONFERENCES

San Francisco Writers Conference -- www.sfwriters.org/

Maui Writers Conference -- www.mauiwriters.com/

RWA has a yearly national conference and local chapters have regional annual or bi-annual conferences.

The San Francisco Writers Conference is usually in February http://www.sfwriters.org/. You do need to register for the conference to do Speed Dating.

The California Writers Club annual conference: usually March.

Many of the same agents who will be at the San Francisco Writers Conference will be there. http://www.sfpeninsulawriters.com/conference/jlmain.html

REALITY CHECK
Persistence Pays!
Writers need to become rejection proof.

HOW TO FIND APPROPRIATE PUBLISHERS AND AGENTS
Market guides -- annual Writer's Market and Guide to Literary Agents
www.Publishersmarketplace.com
www.writersmarket.com/
www.agentquery.com/
www.anotherealm.com/prededitors/
booktrade.info
www.absolutewrite.com/

Hero's Journey and Plotting

FIVE-POINT PLOT STRUCTURE RESOURCE: *THE WRITER'S BRAINSTORMING KIT*, PAM MCCUTCHEON AND MICHAEL WAITE	HERO'S JOURNEY RESOURCES: *THE HERO WITH A THOUSAND FACES* BY JOSEPH CAMPBELL; *THE WRITER'S JOURNEY* BY CHRISTOPHER VOGLER
A. ORDINARY WORLD	1. ORDINARY WORLD
B. TRIGGER EVENT	2. CALL TO ACTION/CALL TO ADVENTURE
	3. REFUSAL OF THE CALL
	4. MENTOR
	5. ACCEPT THE CALL
C. CHANGE OF PLANS	6. ENTERS THE SPECIAL WORLD: TEST, ALLIES AND ENEMIES
	7. APPROACH THE INMOST CAVE
D. THE BLACK MOMENT	8. CONFRONTATION/ ORDEAL/ VIRTUAL DEATH/ FACE YOUR DEMONS
E. RESOLUTION	9. REWARD
	10. THE ROAD BACK
	11. PURIFICATION/ TRANSFORMATION/ RESURRECTION
	12. TRIUMPH/ RETURN TO COMMUNITY WITH THE GIFT

Bibliography

MYTH AND THE HERO'S JOURNEY
Campbell, Joseph. *The Hero With a Thousand Faces*
Campbell, Joseph. *The Power of Myth*
Estés, Clarissa Pinkola. *Women Who Run With The Wolves*
Vogler, Christopher. *The Writer's Journey*

PUBLISHING
Herman, Jeff, *Write the Perfect Book Proposal: 10 That Sold and Why*, 2nd Edition
Howry, Michelle, *Agents, Editors and You: The Insider's Guide to Getting Your Book Published*, Writers Market Library
Larsen, Michael, *Literary Agents: What They Do, How They Do It, and How to Find and Work with the Right One for You, Revised and Expanded*
Lyon, Elizabeth, *Nonfiction Book Proposals Anybody Can Write (Revised and Updated)*
Maisel, Eric, *The Art of the Book Proposal*
Page, Susan, *Shortest Distance Between You and a Published Book*
Rabiner, Susan and Fortunato, Alfred, *Thinking Like Your Editor: How to Write Great Serious Nonfiction--and Get It Published*
Sambuchino, Chuck. *Guide to Literary Agents 2008*
Whalin, W. Terry, *Book Proposals That Sell*

PLOTTING
Atchity, Kenneth and Wong, Chi-Li. *Writing Treatments that Sell: How to Create and Market Your Story Ideas to the Motion Picture and TV Industry*. Henry Holt and Company: New York, c 1997.

Dixon, Deb, GMC: *Goal, Motivation and Conflict*, Gryphon Books
for Writers, c. 200x. www.gryphonbooksforwriters.com

Kercheval, Jesse Lee. *Building Fiction: How to Develop Plot and
Structure*. The University of Wisconsin Press: Madison,
Wisconsin, c. 1997. www.wisc.edu/wisconsinpress

McCutcheon, Pam and Waite, Michael. *The Writer's Brainstorming
Kit, Gryphon Books for Writers.* c. 2001.
www.gryphonbooksforwriters.com

Schmidt Victoria Lynn, Ph. D. *Story Structure Architect*. Writer's
Digest Books. c2005.

Tobias, Ronald B. *20 Master Plots (and How to Build Them)*. Writer's
Digest Books: Cincinnati, Ohio, c. 1993.

About the Author

Who Beth Barany helps are writers and those who want to write. She helps writers enjoy the writing process AND get their projects done.

A Certified Creativity Coach, Beth is also the author of the e-book, *Overcome Writer's Block: 10 Writing Sparks to Ignite Your Creativity*, Beth is the senior editor to the anthology, *Writing Romance: The Ultimate Guide on Craft, Creation, and Industry Connections*. Additionally, Beth has been published in the *Psychic Reader*, the *Paris Free Voice, January Magazine* and *Creativity Calling: The Newsletter of the Creativity Coaching Association*. She's online at http://www.bethbarany.com, and email: beth@bethbarany.com.

After working in journalism for 15 years, and teaching ESL in the US and France, Beth switched her writing focus to fiction, and now writes young adult fantasy. Her young adult fantasy novel, THE DRAGON STONE, is under consideration by agents and editors.

Beth has a bachelor's degree from the University of California, Berkeley, and has started a Masters at the Université Paris VII in Paris History. Additionally, she's received an Advanced Certification in Teaching English as Foreign Language (TEFL), and has studied with Eric Maisel for Creativity Coaching.

On her off-hours, Beth enjoys walking, the outdoors, gardening, art galleries, watching movies, cafes, and reading. Beth is married to singer/song-writer and *handsome* high school physics teacher, Ezra Barany.

LaVergne, TN USA
10 January 2010
169437LV00004B/1/P